NOT WITHOUT HONOR

NOT
WITHOUT
HONOR

THE NAZI POW JOURNAL
OF STEVE CARANO

WITH ACCOUNTS BY
JOHN C. BITZER AND BILL BLACKMON

EDITED BY KAY SLOAN

The University of Arkansas Press
Fayetteville
2008

ISBN-10: 1-55728-884-4
ISBN-13: 978-1-55728-884-4

12 11 10 09 08   5 4 3 2 1

Designed by Liz Lester

⊛ The paper used in this publication meets the minimum requirements of the American National Standard for Permanence of Paper for Printed Library Materials Z39.48-1984.

LIBRARY OF CONGRESS CATALOGING-IN-PUBLICATION DATA

Carano, Steve.
    Not without honor : the Nazi POW journal of Steve Carano : with accounts by John C. Bitzer and Bill Blackmon / edited by Kay Sloan.
        p.   cm.
    Includes bibliographical references and index.
    ISBN-13: 978-1-55728-884-4 (cloth : alk. paper)
    ISBN-10: 1-55728-884-4 (cloth : alk. paper)
    1. Carano, Steve. 2. Stalag XVII B Krems-Gneixendorf. 3. World War, 1939–1945—Prisoners and prisons, German. 4. World War, 1939–1945—Personal narratives, American. 5. Prisoners of war—United States—Diaries. 6. Prisoners of war—Germany—Diaries. I. Bitzer, John C. II. Blackmon, Bill. III. Sloan, Kay. IV. Title.
    D805.5.S737C37   2008
    940.54'72092—dc22
    [B]   2008026889

This book is dedicated to my uncle,
William F. Davidge.

Those who lived before us, who struggled for justice and suffered injustice before us, have not melted into the dust, and have not disappeared. They are with us still. The lives they lived hold us steady . . . Their courage and love evoke our own.

—Kathleen McTigue,
"They Are With Us Still"

Contents

Foreword by Lewis Carlson   ix

Preface   xiii

Acknowledgments   xix

PART ONE
CLAUDIO "STEVE" CARANO'S WARTIME LOG

Introduction   5

Dedication   20

The Wire   21

Holland   25

Life in the Prison Camp   37

Jerry Warning   43

Escape Letter to Rose Carano   44

Six Months a Prisoner of War   46

The Story of Slim Lassiter   48
     Not Without Honor   48
     Paris Prison   61

Joe Hafer   65

Writing by Comrades   66
     What a Price to Pay   67
     A Kriegie's Reply   68
     The Flea Epic   69

"Kurt" Kurtenbach   71

Father Kane   73

Poetry   76

Kriegie Everyday Talk   88

"They Fly for Dollars"   91

About the War   95

Liberation Account   97

Letter from Dutch Nurses   99

Appendix: Carano's Comrades   101

PART TWO
JOHN BITZER'S WARTIME LOG

Introduction   107

Wartime Log   113

Poetry   116

PART THREE
BILL BLACKMON'S STORY

Bill Blackmon   129

Afterword   147

Further Readings   151

Index   157

FOREWORD

Americans do not see former prisoners of war as they do other veterans. Somehow, becoming a POW, as one general put it, "is a failed mission." Even more insensitive was the wife who wrote her husband in a German prison camp, "I still love you even if you are a coward and a prisoner." No hometown parades awaited former prisoners, who were quickly forgotten by their government, the media, and the general public; but their incarceration never leaves them. Several decades after the fact, a psychiatrist asked a former POW, "When were you captured and incarcerated?" His answer was painfully simple: "Last night."

Of the more than ninety-five thousand Americans who became prisoners of the Germans in World War II, 32,730 were Army Air Force personnel shot down over enemy territory. Although the first American air raid over Germany took place July 4, 1942, not until the 1943 Casablanca Conference did British and American leaders design a massive air campaign to destroy the infrastructure of the Third Reich and crush the morale of the German people. The resulting damage was devastating, but those dropping the bombs also suffered enormous casualties. During the October 14, 1943, raid on the Schweinfurt Ball Bearing Works, the Germans shot down sixty B-17 bombers carrying more than five hundred airmen. Some of the daylight bombings of Berlin were even more deadly.

With casualties so common, the possibility of capture was not alien to the pilots and their crews, but most did not anticipate the hostile reception that often awaited them on the ground. Called *Luftgangster* (air gangsters) and paid mercenaries by the German press, German civilians were encouraged to take matters into their own hands when these airmen fell out of the skies, especially after SS Commander Heinrich Himmler assured them, "It is not the task of the police to intervene in altercations between Germans and landed English and American *Terrorflieger* [terror fliers] who have bailed out."

There was little in a man's training to prepare him for the shock of captivity. One moment he was ostensibly an independent force fighting for his country. The next he was reduced to a helpless object at the mercy of his enemies. As one newly captured prisoner put it, "You suddenly realize that by passing from the right side of the front to the wrong you have become a nonentity in the huge business of war." Often disoriented and feeling an element of shame about the capture itself, as well as guilt for having survived when so many of his buddies had not, the new prisoner faced a most uncertain future. He also had to contend with aggressive interrogations, followed by a dangerous and debilitating train ride before finally reaching a permanent prison camp.

Why some prisoners of war survived captivity better than others cannot be explained simply in terms of mental and physical strength. Serendipity played a significant role, especially if the captive had been wounded or became ill shortly after his capture. But by far the most important factor was whether his captors adhered to the 1929 Geneva Convention, which governed all aspects of military captivity, including interrogations, quantity and quality of food, clothing, housing, medical care, allowable punishments, and periodic inspections by the International Red Cross. It was no accident that less than 2 percent of American POWs held by the Germans died in captivity, and many of these from natural causes. In sharp contrast was the 40 percent death rate suffered by Americans held by the Japanese. Simply put, Germany recognized the Geneva Convention; Japan did not. As Claudio "Steve" Carano points out in his journal, the Geneva Convention "protected us against the atrocities inflicted upon other nationalities."

The International Red Cross not only inspected the camps but also oversaw the delivery of food parcels, without which many more prisoners would have died during the last year of the war, as the narratives of Carano, John C. Bitzer, and William H. Blackmon make clear. The International Red Cross and the Young Men's Christian Association also delivered recreational equipment that helped ease the tedium of incarceration, as well as the notebooks and writing and drawing materials that made the lives of these three men more tolerable.

The bane of a POW's existence was boredom and loneliness, which meant that friendships were very important for men desperately needing to retain a sense of well-being. "Initially," said one former POW, "you tended to become very selfish because you spent so much time thinking about yourself and your predicament. It was only when we got beyond that and started doing things for other people that we became less depressed." Blackmon makes it clear how much he valued the friendship and positive attitude of Carano, as did many other men in Stalag XVII B.

There were, of course, moments when a prisoner just had to lower the curtain and be alone with his thoughts, to seclude himself in his own little world. At times this might even involve counting the barbs on the fence that entrapped him, as Carano describes so well in his essay "The Wire." But Carano and his friends never succumbed to something called "barb-wire psychosis," when men literally turned their heads to the wall, gave up, and died. The key to survival for these men was not to be totally preoccupied with a single action or thought, whether it was yourself, your mother's chocolate cake, or counting the barbs on the wire.

Former POWs have more to teach us than simply survival techniques. As Kay Sloan points out in her superb Afterword, "Theirs was not a tale of glorified heroics, but a story of keeping body, mind, and soul alive under grueling uncertainty and tedium—a heroism of the spirit that is often forgotten." The narratives of Steve Carano, John Bitzer, and Bill Blackmon are moving testaments to human possibilities. As one of their fellow prisoners put it, "All people in positions of responsibility, politicians particularly, should have been schooled in the skills of being a good POW. It causes you to look after yourself being aware that someone else is looking out for himself and you mustn't damage him. You are, after all, both equal when all is said and done." Noble words, indeed, for all human beings.

Lewis H. Carlson
Professor Emeritus of History
Western Michigan University

PREFACE

In the spring of 2000, I arrived in Fort Lauderdale for a visit with my sister and her family. On her dining room table a book lay open, revealing carefully handwritten pages and drawings. My brother-in-law was setting up his camera to photograph each yellowed page. This was my introduction to Claudio Stefano Carano's wartime journal from Stalag XVII B. The Carano family, who lived nearby, had trusted my sister with the precious journal so it could be preserved in slides.

The meticulously penned entries and detailed illustrations intrigued me, with their revelations of life from inside one of World War II's most well-known prison camps, the basis for the long-running television comedy *Hogan's Heroes* and the serious film and play *Stalag 17*. Most of all, the faces that Carano sketched—somber, chiseled-looking faces of soldiers in captivity—piqued my curiosity. Who were these men? How had they managed to survive the ordeal of capture? The journal itself was one answer. S. Sgt. Carano had used these pages as a private space in a public life, a way of focusing his energy, his art, and his thoughts in the brutal eighteen months he spent in Stalag XVII. Yet his journal was not only the creation of a single individual; it also provided a source of community for the prisoners, evidenced by the poems, cartoons, and stories that his comrades had written for its pages. From *POW WOW,* a newspaper put together by a group of daring POWs in Stalag Luft III B and distributed through several camps, Carano also drew essays and wrote or copied poems, compiling them into his journal if the words were particularly moving or consoling.

The Red Cross sent out the blank, bound books, printed by the YMCA, together with colored pencils, and the combination fired the imagination of imprisoned GIs looking for ways to distract themselves from hunger, cold, and loneliness. In German prison camps across Europe, American POWs made good use of the books and some of the results can be found on prisoner of war websites. At Stalag Luft I in Barth, on the Baltic Sea near Berlin, Charles Early, a lieutenant from South Carolina, drew lively colored cartoons in his book, poking fun at Germans and POWs alike. For Robert Swartz, the book became an ongoing letter to his family in Michigan, filled with the details that the POW's censored correspondence would not allow. Aaron Kuptsow recorded his days in a barrack where Jewish POWs had been segregated from the other Americans, even scribbling down recipes such as "Kriegie Pie" (named for the German slang word for prisoner of war), made of a concoction of prunes, margarine and biscuits—ingredients found in the Red Cross parcels. In another part of the camp, John Cordner, a Royal Air Force navigator, sketched the barren landscape outside the barracks and wrote poetry in his own YMCA journal, which he titled "Kriegie Days" in decorative script across the cover.

Carano's own book stands as an example of record keeping, artistry, cartoons, and a collaborative forum for the literary expressions of his comrades. It exemplifies the way the individual POWs put their stamps on the journals, allowing them a space to reflect, a space that they could "own" in an environment that stood to threaten their sense of selfhood. Like one of the many tunnels the men dug beneath the barracks, the journal was a private place that they could share, another place where they could be a team conspiring to keep hope alive. In the making of the journal, they found not the freedom of the Austrian Alps beyond Stalag XVII, but another kind of freedom, found in the irrepressible urge to create, to shape the world around them according to their words, drawings, and even recipes made of the most rudimentary ingredients. The act of writing and drawing itself was a self-affirmation, and the medium provided by the journal is nearly as significant as the messages within its covers.

While flying bomb raids over Europe, the men had relied keenly on one another, learning the nuances of each other's personality, temperament, and expertise. Grounded and in captivity, that same sense of being part of a team helped them to keep their spirits and even their humor. In camp, the selfish men were the ones held in greatest contempt, and looking out for one another became a central ethos.

As I talked with Carano's widow, Rose, his son, Steve, and his daughter-in-law, Cathy, I felt the powerful personality of the artist and writer who had created that journal, bound with even stitches in the brown cloth of his uniform. Soon I contacted one of his closest surviving comrades, William H. Blackmon, known as "Blackie" in the pages of Carano's journal, and found even more stories about survival during this darkest of wars. Blackmon, who could sometimes joke and laugh about his experiences in Stalag XVII, never joked about the Louisiana orphanage where he'd spent over five years of his boyhood. Those were terrible days, a time that seemed to prepare him for the atrocities and hardships of the prison camp before liberation came in the spring of 1945.

I felt a personal connection to Bill Blackmon as I listened to his recollections about life as a POW in World War II. My own uncle, William F. Davidge, had also been a prisoner of war, but, like so many other veterans, he had always chosen to keep his memories to himself. My older sister remembers the warm June day in 1945 when our uncle, T. Sgt. Bill Davidge, came home from the war after sixteen months as a prisoner of the Germans. While she sat playing on the front steps of our grandparents' home in Hattiesburg, Mississippi, a tall, blond stranger leapt over her as he bounded up the stairs to the front porch. She could not comprehend that she was seeing her uncle, a bone-thin prisoner of war finally returning to the home he had dreamed of during captivity at the hands of the Nazis. Instead of calling his parents, he had decided to surprise them by arriving in a taxi that rolled to a stop before the frame house on Hattiesburg's Mabel Avenue. When his teenaged younger sister, Pat, opened the screened door, he was finally home from a journey that had taken him through the nightmares of history's worst war.

But though Bill Davidge had left the war, the war never left him. He had been a young man of nineteen and the chief engineer on one of the B-17s flying dangerous daylight raids over Nazi-held Europe. During a mission on February 6, 1944, German flak struck his plane, the "Old Man," killing the pilot and navigator as they flew over a village south of Paris called Wissous. Determined to spare the townspeople below, the copilot, Lt. Arthur L. Clark, ordered the crew to bail out while he struggled to avoid crashing the "Old Man" into the center of Wissous. Trying to escape the chaos on board, Bill Davidge managed to clip on his parachute, but his boot caught in the door as he jumped out, leaving him swinging helplessly from the plane's underbelly as it descended rapidly toward earth. Certain of his doom, he suddenly felt a hand grab his trapped foot and release it, freeing him from the grip of the door. As he floated to the ground in his parachute, he saw Lt. Clark crash-land the flaming bomber in a park.

On the ground on that cold February day in Wissous, a fifteen-year-old French boy named Claude Sene and his mother heard the terrible roar of the falling plane directly overhead and thought surely it would crash on their home. Instead, young Claude watched as its wings angled nearly vertically toward the church across the street, almost slicing the steeple. When a plume of smoke rose from the park, he raced to the site where the wreckage burned and found the bodies of four young airmen barely older than he. Decades later, an elderly Monsieur Sene described the scene to my daughter and me at a commemoration in Wissous in February 2006, tears filling his eyes as he recited the names of the dead and their ages, in their late teens or early twenties. Of the ten aboard the "Old Man," six crewmen had survived.

German soldiers captured my uncle soon after he landed. For decades, he kept his memories of the war and his captivity privately locked in his mind. After the fiftieth anniversary of the war's end, he found an invitation from a citizen of Wissous, Madame Pierette Rembur, who was organizing a commemoration for the American airmen who had crashed outside her village on that winter day in 1944. He returned to a hero's welcome in Wissous, where a stone pillar now marks the site of the crash. The memory of the flaming plane and his crewmates haunted him, and he had expressed it in his silence for many years. But after his visit to Wissous, he finally began to record his memories of the time when he was a nineteen-year-old farm boy from Mississippi, marched in hellish conditions from one detention center near the Baltic to another in southern Germany as the war neared its close, then finally on a "death march" when six thousand prisoners marched more than six hundred miles in the deadly cold months during Europe's worst winter on record.

The town of Wissous hosts an annual memorial service in the small Catholic church that would have been destroyed by the B-17, had not Arthur Clark struggled to crash in a nearby park instead. There, attending for my uncle in 2006, I met a veteran named John C. Bitzer, a former POW from Cleveland whose own B-17 had been shot down north of Paris on December 30, 1943. A ball turret gunner, he was the last man to escape before his plane exploded in a ball of fire. During our conversation, I discovered that he, like Steve Carano, had recorded poetry and drawings in a YMCA "Wartime Log" while incarcerated in Stalag Luft VI and Stalag IV, Lager D.

Bitzer's own narrative begins where Carano's leaves off: with his liberation on April 28, 1945, after the nearly three-month death march through snowy Prussian fields that my uncle, too, had survived. Bitzer's entries—including drawings and poetry—follow the Carano log in the pages of this book. While one man chose to record the endurance of captivity, the other was inspired to write by the joy of liberation. For my uncle, it was the passage of fifty years and the compassion of his new friends in Wissous that freed him to share a few of his memories. Even then, he preferred to write them rather than talk about those brutal months.

This work belongs to them but it is for us, later generations who have so much to learn from the experiences of those who endured the horrors of World War II. For themselves, they had the desire to forget. For us, they had the duty to remember.

K. S.

ACKNOWLEDGMENTS

Without the generosity and enthusiasm of the Carano family, this project would never have made it to fruition. Rose Carano graciously invited me into her apartment in Plantation, Florida, showing me photographs and letters from her husband written while he was at war or in Stalag XVII B. Her son, Steve Carano, and his wife, Cathy, were instrumental in giving me access to letters and documents relevant to the project. In a telephone interview from New York, Hugo Carano, the brother of Claudio "Steve" Carano, deepened my understanding of his family's artistic background and his brother's bravery. The grandchildren, Steve, Jean, and Mary, helped me photograph loose pages in the journal, sharing stories about their grandfather as we worked.

Rose Carano also helped me locate her husband's comrade, Bill Blackmon, a fellow POW in Stalag XVII. I found Bill living in Baton Rouge and interviewed him several times, discovering one of the best Southern raconteurs I've met. He possesses an exceptional memory for people and events, and he generously gave me a wealth of information in records, photographs, and stories. Through our long conversations and visits I have made a new friend, and to him I am deeply grateful.

When I met John and Marion Bitzer at a POW commemoration in Wissous, France, in February 2006, I learned that John Bitzer had kept his own World War II YMCA Wartime Log after he was captured by the Germans in 1944. His journal entries begin at liberation, the moment when Carano had stopped. John sent me a copy of his Log Book, and Marion tucked in her "two cents' worth," as she called it, which was a copy of the powerful speech that John had made in 2001 to the Rotary Club in Cleveland, Ohio. All of it revealed a different wartime experience from that of Steve Carano. I met the Bitzers when Mme. Pierett Rembur opened her home to us all in Wissous, providing a place where Americans and Europeans could come together in appreciation of our past alliances and of American sacrifice in World War II. With her energy and determination, she was instrumental in establishing the town's annual commemoration for the ten young American soldiers whose bomber crashed just beyond the village limits of Wissous on February 6, 1944. So successful is the Wissous commemoration that other POWs such as John Bitzer, who crashed in a nearby area later, now attend.

Through Sandra and Bill Doepp and Amy Boltz—my sister, brother-in-law, and niece—I came to know about the Carano manuscript. Spread on their dining table in Florida, with Bill's sophisticated camera equipment focused above the pages, the manuscript was first introduced to me. I'm especially indebted to Bill, a professional photographer, for his expert help on this project and the long hours he spent meticulously photographing not only the journal pages but letters and articles saved by Steve and Rose Carano while he was in Stalag XVII B.

Robert E. Mathis, my uncle and a World War II Army veteran of the Pacific battles, gave me invaluable perspectives on the war's effect upon his generation. Though never a POW, his impressive encyclopedic knowledge of the war, both from his own experience as a ground soldier and from his extensive reading and research, gave me useful direction on this project. In addition, Verne Woods, a POW in Stalag Luft I, gave me information about his crewmate, Roke Lieberman, who led Jewish services in Stalag XVII B.

Miami University funded a leave that provided me the opportunity to advance this manuscript toward publication, a portion of which first appeared as an article in *American History*. While teaching at the Miami University Dolibois European Center in Luxembourg, I heard a panel of European survivors of World War II: Joseph Schlang, Rene Kerschen, Jean Majerus, Aloise Raths, and Pierce Pixius, all young men when they were imprisoned by the Germans for either their resistance or their ethnicity. Listening to their testimonies was a powerful experience, as they opened their histories to my students and revealed the suffering and bravery endured by so many. Paul Dostert, the director of the Resistance Documentation Center, provided historical information prior to the question and answer period, and Professor Emile Haag and Dr. Ekkehard Stiller, dean of the center, arranged the presentation.

Larry Malley, editor and friend, provided his guidance and editorial wisdom yet again in our work together on this project. Lewis Carlson's ideas, scholarship, and expertise about prisoners of war provided me guidance and help toward the end of this project.

My husband, David Schloss, and my daughter, Signe Schloss, have offered me support throughout the progress of this book. They have my heartfelt thanks.

Finally, my uncle, Bill Davidge, ultimately provided the reason for my taking on this project. On a beautiful April day in France in 1987, my mother and I stood in a park in Wissous near a monument marking the spot where her brother's plane had crashed in 1944, leaving him to be captured by the Nazis. "He was only nineteen," she whispered, with tears in her eyes. I knew little of my uncle's experience, only that it was so painful he, like so many other World War II veterans, rarely talked about the war. All over Europe, I had seen the physical scars left by that horrific war. I had heard the painful silence of my uncle, broken only by the briefest of allusions to his wartime experiences. Once, he told us how a naïve young woman had reacted when he told her that he was just home from the war, a former POW. "But they treated you well, didn't they?" she asked. He shook his head in disbelief. "It was terrible," he told her, but refused to say more. When I read John Bitzer's accounts of the war crimes he had endured as a young POW—the "Baltic Cruise," the "Heydekrug Run" and an eighty-six day death march in the freezing Prussian cold—I sent them to my uncle since they bore some resemblance to the fragments of stories he had slowly disclosed over the decades. "Yes," he responded. "Unfortunately I was a part of what you listed. You are doing what I wanted to do, and am capable of doing, but could not bear to relive the bad memories. I want my family to know from you what I, and other boys, did for them." This book is dedicated to him, and to all of those heroic "other boys."

NOT WITHOUT HONOR

PART ONE

CLAUDIO "STEVE" CARANO'S WARTIME LOG

When the war temblor ends, and the dust settles, and the actual truth is known, the horrors of it will strike us like a tidal wave.

—FROM THE JOURNAL OF
CLAUDIO "STEVE" CARANO

Introduction

On a warm July evening in 1942, Claudio Stefano Carano came home from his job as foreman at a mannequin factory in Brooklyn. He was tired but happy, ready to take his wife, Rose, out dancing at their favorite club, Coney Island Nights. She was good at the two-step and had even won prizes doing a fast dance called the Peabody, and he liked to show her off in the contests. Tonight, though, they would probably sit it out during the fast ones. Rose was pregnant, with the baby due in August. That day, after he'd sold some mannequins at Wanamaker's Store, he had picked up a box of chocolates to surprise her.

A terrible war was raging across the Atlantic and in the Pacific jungles, and sometimes it seemed that the world beyond America was on fire, consuming the conversations of young men with talk about enlistment and the draft. Carano's younger brother, Hugo, was already in the Marine Corps, on his way to the Pacific. On that night, though, his thoughts turned to the son he hoped he would soon have, and the things he would teach him: baseball, for one thing, the way he played with his own two younger brothers in the high school ball park near Eighteenth Street in Brooklyn. He was a natural athlete, a strong and tough daredevil. Once, sliding into third base, he'd broken his leg in two places.

He would be a good father, he knew, as long as he followed the example set by his own dad. Stefano Carano, an Italian immigrant from Bologna, had impressed upon his three sons and two daughters that America had given the family great opportunities, a chance to prosper that they would not have had in their native Italy. He and his brother Vincent, both sculptors, had done well in their new country, working in the mannequin industry and with the U.S. Bronze Company, where Vincent had hand-molded the faces of Babe Ruth and Lou Gehrig for the plaques that are still embedded in the grass of Yankee Stadium's center field. At home, Stefano insisted that the family speak English and not Italian. To honor their new country, he taught his children the traditional values of hard work and patriotism.

The war was never far from anyone's mind, and that afternoon as Carano took off his jacket and kissed his wife, he knew from the look in her eyes that something was wrong as she handed him a cream-colored postcard. Tension worked his jaw as he read the words that he had half expected would come: "Greetings. Your friends and neighbors have selected you for service in the Armed Forces . . ." But despite any misgivings he had, he remembered the strong sense of duty to the United States that his father had instilled in him.

At age twenty-one, Carano ["the name's Steve," he quickly informed anyone who made the mistake of calling him "Claudio"] was a man of fierce loyalties to his family and his country. He couldn't imagine saying goodbye to Rose. But on August 5, when she was in her ninth month of pregnancy, the Army assigned him to the base in Atlantic City, a bus trip of three and a half hours from home. When his son was born soon after, Carano slipped off twice to find his wife in the hospital and see his baby, named Stephen. Soon he was shipped to gunnery school in Scotfield, Illinois—too far away to take a bus home. But nothing could diminish Carano's stubborn, independent streak. He knew what he wanted and went after it, and he knew how to take the consequences.

A handsome man with a cocky smile and a debonair moustache, Carano possessed an intensity and self-confidence that impressed his officers and his comrades alike. Despite a fiery temper, he had an unusual ability to wrangle his way out of tough situations and smooth-talk his commanders. "He sure could talk his way out of jams," remembered one of his comrades, Bill Blackmon. "He knew how to finagle, I tell you. Steve had two or three A-2 jackets, the leather jacket that the gunners wore. He could go in the supply room and talk that guy out of anything he wanted. Steve was just good at everything. Women, too."

It was the sort of cunning that would serve Carano well in his eighteen months of incarceration in Stalag XVII.

Carano and Blackmon met during flight training in Dalhart, Texas, and it was there that Carano, older than Blackmon by four years, took the younger man under his wing like a brother. Blackmon, raised in a Louisiana orphanage from the time he was eight years old until he ran away at age thirteen, had never enjoyed the kind of close family bonds that united the Caranos. "I loved him like a brother," said Blackmon, looking back on the friendship more than sixty years later. And Carano did look out after "Blackie," as he nicknamed his tall, skinny eighteen-year-old friend with the heavy Southern accent and big smile.

In the fall of 1943, after their phase training in Texas, Carano shipped off with Blackmon to the Air Force base at Ridgewell, England, to serve in the Eighth Air Force. Stationed in the 535th Bomb Squadron of the renowned 381st Bomb Group, the men were assigned to complete twenty-five bombing missions, after which the Army would release fliers from battle duty to return stateside as instructors. Though some heroic men flew even more than twenty-five, few soldiers ever reached that magic number. During the war, approximately thirty-three thousand Army Air Corps men became prisoners of war of the Germans. The average number of missions was eight, and after that a soldier felt he was running on borrowed time, counting himself lucky to survive "the hump," the midway mark of twelve or thirteen runs.

As a radioman, Carano would crawl into the plane through the waist along with the gunners. Inside, he took his position toward the front of the B-17, behind the pilot and copilot, headgear in place, and faced his radio sets. Above him was his gun, on a swivel. Like other radio operators, Carano had been trained to avoid the false signals sent out by the Germans. In combat, he used the interphone to inform the rest of the crew about what was happening. He knew that, in a crisis, a calm voice was a crucial source of trust and assurance for embattled men, and Carano was good at conveying the confidence that came naturally to him. "He was the best," said Blackmon. "Some of them showed their nerves, you know, but not Steve." His interphone was one of the most important devices on the ship during a fight.

In 1943, when Carano and Blackmon flew their missions, small fighter planes escorted the bombers a few hundred miles inside enemy territory before turning back to refuel, leaving the B-17s on their own to face the German flak and fighters. Other dangers besides enemy fire plagued the men. When the aircraft climbed to high altitudes, temperatures plunged to sixty or seventy degrees below zero. In that bitter cold, wind whistling through their helmets, their breath condensed on oxygen masks, sometimes freezing the mask to their cheeks and causing frostbite. An airman could pass out if he neglected to put on his oxygen mask in time, or to properly adjust it. The life that may have seemed romantic and glamorous to the young soldiers training in the States—or to the British women they met in Ridgewell—became a brutal and dangerous reality.

As losses climbed, tension and grief escalated. The men conducted daring daytime air battles with the Luftwaffe, flying deep into the heart of Nazi Germany to bomb industrial targets. But when comrades failed to return, they often sought quiet places to weep or curse in solitude. The men at Ridgewell blew off steam in British clubs, finding a kind of alternate reality with young women, good food, and dancing. Two worlds existed side by side for the young flying men of the Eighth Army, and sometimes they wondered which was real and which was dream: the nightmarish world in the sky with cities going up in flames and burning B-17s spiraling down to the earth, or the flirtatious laughter of young women in a smoky pub at night. But the rising death toll of their comrades was a constant reminder that the flak and blazing planes were real.

The B-17 was designed to fly high, with a cruising speed of about 170 miles per hour, as pilots flew over Germany in broad daylight to conduct bombing raids. The British thought the Americans were crazy to conduct such daring missions without cover of darkness. Fast as it was, the unescorted "Flying Fortress" was vulnerable to the German fighter attacks as the Luftwaffe became better coordinated and more efficient. When German flak hit the B-17s—a sound, as Carano described it, like a boy running a stick along a corrugated tin building—the plane had a tendency to catch fire. At times the men of the Eighth Air Force, flying in formation, watched helplessly as a nearby B-17, struck by flak, exploded into a ball of flames. They would hold their breath, waiting to see the white parachutes that signaled their comrades' dangerous descent into enemy territory.

Each man had his own way of coping with the danger, whether attending the base's prayer services, saying a rosary, wearing a "lucky" handkerchief or pair of socks, or surrounding himself with young British women at night.

For Bill Blackmon, the Army's organized prayer services offered no solace, and he politely resisted even when the chaplain personally invited him to attend. The forced religious services during his years in the orphanage made him chafe at the thought. "The Matron gave us a penny in an envelope with our names on it, to put in the box at prayer services," Blackmon remembered. "We'd be in for a beating if we lost that penny. Somehow, I just never went for religion after that. Not the organized kind, anyway."

Going out on the town with Carano was a good distraction from the life-risking missions of the day, especially since Carano always seemed to find the prettiest women. The British women liked him so much that other soldiers were jealous, but the independent streak that women found attractive led to trouble with the Army in England. Twice Carano stayed in town too long on a pass with his romantic escapades, coming back to his barrack in the rain of early British mornings. This time—unlike his AWOL to see his infant son in Brooklyn—the Army didn't look the other way. He lost his Tech stripes and was sent to the stockade.

"He never talked about those women," reported Blackmon, "even though you'd always see him out in bars with a couple of the most beautiful ones. He had that charm, you know. That moustache. But it was his wife Rose and his young son that he talked about. They were the ones he loved."

On missions, Carano found another way of coping: he took charge, crisply asking each member of the crew if he was OK. Not one to easily show fear, he kept his comrades' spirits up. "He'd be in that radio room when we were going on a mission," said Blackmon, "and he'd always come back there and see that everything was all right. 'Blackie, you doin' all right?' He'd holler back to the tail to the guy back there, let everybody know he cared about us." They were a team and he was a natural at building morale, perhaps not unlike the way he would urge on his teammates on the beloved baseball fields that had been such an important part of Carano's civilian life. Every man depended on the others, each man's actions affected the whole group. But this time, winning was everything.

"Steve was fiery and wasn't scared. He had a temper that must have seen him through the war. One minute he'd be chewing you out and then you'd turn around and he'd be lovin' you to death, put his arm around your shoulders . . . he used to get on me all the time, I got used to it. I'd been around him so long, since Texas. He'd get mad at something, but then he'd get over it fast. Like I said, I loved that guy to death, I really did." Blackmon paused, remembering, and then continued. "I never saw him turn ashen and pale like some of the men when we'd get hit up in the air. Some of them looked scared to death, especially if they had kids. The only way they could get back home was to get busted for refusing to fly, and lose stripes, and nobody wanted to do that."

On the morning of December 1, 1943, nearly two years after the bombing of Pearl Harbor had launched the United States into the war, Carano started out on his third mission out of Ridgewell, this time as the replacement radioman on a B-17 in a bombing raid over Leverkusen, Germany.

"He was chosen because he was so good," remembered Bill Blackmon. Yet somehow, that morning, an apprehension about flying came over Carano; he wrote that he had "an expectant feeling . . . the moment I was told I would fly the mission as a spare radio operator on a strange crew."

Like many other daring raids by the Eighth Air Force out of Ridgewell, the flight successfully conducted its mission but ended tragically. With German flak repeatedly hitting the plane, the pilot managed to find his way back to the North Sea, but then went down in the water off the Holland coast. Carano survived the crash and, after being rescued by the Dutch, soon found himself surrounded by Nazi occupiers. In New York, Rose received a telegram informing her that her husband was missing in action. Soon after, the telephone rang. It was a stranger, assuring her that Steve was alive. He had heard it over his ham radio, and he wanted to let her know that she was not a widow. Later, the Army learned that Carano had been captured in Holland.

When the military sent Rose Carano her husband's personal effects after his capture, she found love letters from British nurses among the clothing and shaving supplies. Despite the hurt, she was able to shrug it off. "He loved me and I loved him, but he was lonely," she said. "And it was a dangerous time. Besides, that was just in his blood." As Carano was recovering from his wounds in a German hospital, he wrote his wife that the nurses were so nice to him that he wanted her to buy clothes—skirts, stockings and sweaters—to send them as thank you gifts from America. He enclosed their sizes so she could do the shopping in Brooklyn's stores. He'd been boasting to the Germans about the American way of life, and now he wanted Rose to help him prove it to the nurses.

Carano's self-confidence and tough spirit undoubtedly helped him survive eighteen months as a prisoner of war in Stalag XVII, sprawled at the foot of the Alps near Krems, Austria. Though his formal education went only as far as grade school, he was a quick learner, picking up enough German to communicate with the guards. He soon learned the German word for prisoners of war: Kriegsgefangene, or "Kriegies." Lice and bedbugs crawled in the palliases where they slept and maggots floated in the thin gruel that kept them alive. As Bill Blackmon recalls, "The worms looked exactly like the bits of barley except for the tiny black heads on them. I spent my first day of incarceration picking these worms out of the soup, but later realized we were getting protein from the worms."

Yet on the other side of the wire was a reminder that they were comparatively fortunate: there, the Russian prisoners looked like skeletons shivering in rags. If the Americans tried to toss Red Cross cigarettes or a chocolate "D-bar" to them across the wire, the German guards instantly shot down the desperate Russians who tried to retrieve the precious items. When the guards weren't looking, the Russians, forced to work in the nearby fields, would toss a stolen potato or even a hand-carved trinket such as a cigarette holder over the fence in exchange for tobacco. More than three million Russians died in German camps because of Stalin's refusal to recognize the Geneva Convention, and also because of Hitler's hatred for what he saw as "half-witted Mongols." American "Kriegies" knew that the Geneva Convention had saved them from those torturous conditions. Carano wrote of his gratitude for those regulations, "which protected us against the atrocities inflicted upon other nationalities."

Several months after his arrival at the camp in January 1944, as the cold Austrian winter was giving way to spring, Carano watched as a new group of captured fliers straggled into the camp. Among them he spotted the blond-haired, lanky figure of his buddy, "Blackie" Blackmon, looking bedraggled as he made his way to Barracks 29A, set up for new prisoners. Carano ran at him and jubilantly clapped him on the back as if Blackmon had made a homerun. "You son of a bitch!" he exclaimed. "I knew I'd see you here sooner or later!" He looked up at his comrade's thin face, more seasoned and wary-eyed than he might have remembered. It was more than the fatigue and trauma of the capture. After completing seventeen bomb missions over Europe—one of the last raids was part of the relentless daytime bombardment of Berlin in March of 1944—Blackmon had gone from being a boy to a man in just a few months. His twentieth birthday had been only a few days before his capture.

Blackmon was happy to see a familiar face in that desolate place, especially a friend with a personality like Carano's. "Steve was a man's man," he said. "Everybody liked him. Everybody who came into contact with him liked him. They might have had little arguments with him, but Steve would always win. He had a temper, but it wouldn't be five minutes before he'd be patting you on the back again. He'd do anything in the world for you, he was that type of fellow."

Since Carano lived in a nearby barrack in the same compound, he often invited Blackmon to share a cup of coffee with him. "I used to love to go back there in his bunk, see the things he'd made." Among them was a special cupboard above his bunk, complete with an oil-cloth-like covering so no one could see—and possibly steal—the supplies that Carano had stored there. He had constructed a wooden flap with a knob to conceal the area. Among the contents was coffee, kept in a special container that Carano had made by beating tin cans flat and then remolding them. He had even attached handles on both sides of his special coffee tin. As they drank, they talked about freedom, getting home, and the war. They would wonder if the Russians might bomb the camp, since the fighter planes had hit close several times.

"He made a nice area back in his bunk, and he kept himself neat and clean, I know that," said Blackmon. "Even though that cold water wasn't turned on but twice a day." Always, as they talked, Carano would be tinkering, creating something from the odds and ends that a kriegie might find in the dirt. Once, Carano had a primitive crystal radio set that he'd made by bartering D-bars and Lucky Strike cigarettes for headsets from the guards. Cigarettes and chocolate bars became the currency in the culture that quickly formed in Stalag XVII. The headsets had been stripped from tanks by German guards desperate to support themselves and their families. Clotheslines served as crude but effective antennae, disguised by the laundry hanging from it. In that makeshift fashion, the men could pick up the BBC news to relay to other information-starved POWs. They followed the D-Day invasion on June 4, 1944, the Battle of the Bulge in December of 1944, and the shocking, demoralizing news of the death of President Roosevelt on April 12, 1945. Most of the military reports gave them hope. "Out the gate in '48" was one of their slogans, and a more hopeful one: "Home alive in '45." His Army radio training, when Carano had learned to take apart and reassemble radios, had paid off in unexpected ways.

Sometime after that first winter of 1943–44—one of the coldest recorded in twentieth century Austria—the YMCA packed blank, bound books in the Red Cross shipments to prison camps, along with the usual canned food, sports equipment, and personal supplies for the captives. The YMCA included colored pencils and ink, and for a talented artist and writer like Steve Carano, these gifts were a treasure. Carano allayed his boredom by recording his story in those pages; what resulted was not a day-by-day log of events, but instead a place where he ruminated about his experiences, and allowed his comrades a forum for their poetry, their essays, and even their jokes. He kept the journal carefully stashed in a makeshift cubby in the shadows above his bunk.

Blackmon never saw the journal, which Carano kept for the men in his barrack. But, like an older brother, Carano gave Blackmon advice, even if it wasn't what the younger POW wanted to hear. Upon hearing that Blackmon was digging a tunnel and making plans to escape, Carano shook his head. Don't do it, he warned. Too many risks out there. Where would he go?

Yet at the same time, Carano was secretly making his own plans to escape with two comrades, Charles Bang of Virginia and Carlton Josephson of Connecticut, shot down with him on December 1, 1943. In case he was caught and killed, he had written a letter to Rose and left it with a trusted bunkmate from New York named Charlie Groth. Though he often had shouting matches with Groth back in England ("I'd see 'em just yelling, real loud, at each other," said Bill Blackmon. "They'd be right up in each other's face, and then it would be gone. They'd be arm in arm, walking down the street, best buddies"), Groth was a fellow Brooklynite and Carano knew he could count on Charlie to get his private letter to Rose after the camps were finally liberated. But who knew when that would be?

"One year in a German prison camp," he wrote in that secret letter to Rose during the winter of 1944–45, "is just one year too long to be away from the ones I love, especially yourself and my son who is growing rapidly and forgetting (if ever he knew) that his father really existed." Charlie Groth could tell her, he wrote, about "the way we have to live in this hole." But it wasn't only the terrible conditions or his desire to see his family that inspired him to slip beyond the wires of Stalag XVII. Escape was an assertion of the kind of man he was: "I felt that if I didn't at least try to get home before these damned Germans decide to quit, I don't think that I could ever again feel as though I was half the man I ever considered myself."

Perhaps he feared that too many escapes would jeopardize all the men, or that Blackmon was too young and inexperienced to make it far beyond the wire. At any rate, Carano's own escape never materialized. The guards made him, Josephson and Bang aware that they knew of their escape plans. Someone had informed on them. Again, the uncertainty: who might it have been?

In prison, many soldiers searched for a goal, whether it was escape or something more tangible: long walks around the compound, boxing and playing other sports with the equipment sent by the YMCA, or washing out their dirty clothing. They made routines in their daily lives and found things to accomplish, something to remind them of hope and of their own power and worth. Each barrack, holding more than one hundred men, had its own stories to tell. Many POWs dug tunnels for escape routes, feverishly scooping out the earth with a firm destination in their minds. Looming beyond the camp to the north lay the cold German Alps, but to the west was Switzerland, with its promise of freedom. Other POWs whittled scavenged wood with pieces of tin cans they used as knives, forged crucifixes made of scrounged metal, or bartered instant coffee, cigarettes or D-bars with the guards. Some played in orchestras, with YMCA instruments, and others put on plays, including the authors of the play, *Stalag 17*.

Some, like Carano, sketched or wrote in the pages of the blank journals supplied by the Red Cross and published by the YMCA. Steve Carano took his journal seriously, filling the pages with drawings of his friends' faces, the barracks, common utensils, and recordings of the life around him. Like the best of soldiers, he shared it with his fellow prisoners, carefully copying down their experiences or allowing them to fill a page with sentiments about home or grief about a fallen comrade. Toward the end of his journal, he wrote his own poem about the stories he had recorded.

> Now where did I get these stories? That's what I want to tell.
> They're gathered from my buddies round me, in a German prison cell.
> Some with arms or legs shot off, some who cannot see.
> But every man here has done his part, to preserve Democracy.
> Their fighting days are over, and in my mind there's no doubt
> If everyone would do as much, we'd soon have the Jerry out.

Carano filled his pages with the heroics of men like "Slim" Lassater, who nearly escaped from the Nazis in France before he was captured and sent to Stalag XVII, or the lessons taught by the prison chaplain, Captain Stephen W. Kane, who led services in a thick Irish brogue. For light, Carano had only what the men called a "butter burner," a tin can with a wick designed to burn margarine, which acted like a long-burning candle. In the bitter, windy cold of the barrack, Carano often had to stop and warm his hands over the small flame to keep writing or drawing. Yet when one looks at the meticulous handwriting and the firm lines in the pages of his journal, his pen never seemed to falter as he filled sheet after sheet with beautifully scripted or drawn work. At times—as he contemplated and even planned escape—his patience wavered. The tough Brooklynite found another way of coping in the pages of his journal. It was his gift to history, to his comrades, and to his family.

Always creative, he sewed a cover for the book from his brown uniform, carefully stitching the edges to secure it, making it easier to disguise and hide from intrusive guards or surprise searches from the SS, who seemed especially interested in confiscating log books and diaries. He constructed pockets in the front and back where he could slide other material he wanted to save, such as the German propaganda that the guards gave out and the programs from annual Christmas shows performed by the POWs, sometimes in drag. A couple of those shows were actually caught on camera by a daring Kriegie named Ben Phelper. Phelper, who must have been an ingenuous negotiator with the guards, had managed to trade Red Cross supplies for the inexpensive camera. In 1946, he went on to publish his photographs and commentary in a leather-bound volume titled *Kriegie Memories,* which resembles a very unusual kind of school yearbook. Among his important photographs is a picture of a soldier, a "boy actor," posing in a woman's dress. Such impersonations perhaps made them think of movie stars like Rita Hayworth or Betty Grable, the beautiful women whose pictures had once decorated their Army barracks. "Some of the lads sure did look good when they made up as a girl," wrote Phelper. "One had to look again to be sure they were in the right place." Others, like Bill Blackmon, refused to attend the programs, considering them silly and uncomfortable, but for most they provided grand entertainment, good laughs for at least one evening.

Like Ben Phelper's unique photo record, Steve Carano's journal provides a window into the world of the prisoners of war—men who waged a different war than the one fought on battlefields or in the air. The war that Carano records is deeply personal, involving denunciations of POWs in letters from the home front. His comrades fought for their dignity in the face of letters from fathers and fiancées who, as Carano reported, called them "cowards who allowed themselves to be captured" and told them not to return home. Bill Blackmon recalls a "Dear John" letter written by a young woman to her fiancé in Stalag XVII, in which she wrote that she was going out with a Marine, a "real man who wouldn't give up" by allowing himself to be captured. "She must have gotten about four thousand letters from the men in camp, telling her what they thought of her," he said, an edge of bitterness still in his voice. Carano often refers to the bravery of his comrades, as if he felt the need to remind Americans that great courage was needed to undergo the physical and psychological ordeals in Stalag XVII.

After Carano's release from Stalag XVII during the liberation of May 1945, he left the Army as a Staff Sergeant, still without those Tech stripes he'd left behind in England, and Bill Blackmon never saw or heard from his best friend again. Always the free spirit, Carano departed from the Army so hurriedly that he failed to attend the gathering in which he would have received his Purple Heart and other medals, rushing home to New York and his family instead. Before he had shipped out for the Army in 1942, a Dodgers scout had asked that he try out for the team, but with a knee badly damaged from the war, baseball was no longer an option. Instead, he started his own mannequin manufacturing business and, with Rose, raised their two sons, Steve and Hugo, born in 1947. In later years, when his health began to decline, he and Rose retired to south Florida, where their son Steve lived.

He rarely seemed to look back, never joining the American Ex-Prisoners of War Organization, although periodically he would try to track down his former comrades, especially Bill Blackmon. As the years passed, the trauma and wounds from his battle with the German fighters on that December day in 1943 took their toll on his body. He developed multiple sclerosis and Rose would push him in his wheelchair around the condominium grounds so they could get fresh air together on warm Florida evenings. Even then, he never lost his fighting spirit. Several months after Carano's death in 1996, Bill Blackmon finally located his old friend's phone number, but Rose was the one who answered. She'd heard a lot about "Blackie" over the years but never spoken to him. All Blackmon could think of was how narrowly he had missed finding Carano. He promised Rose he would call back soon, and hung up quickly so she wouldn't hear the tears in his voice.

For decades, Carano's cloth-bound journal lay in a cabinet drawer in the family dining room. On rare occasions, he would pull it out to show to his two sons and later, his five grandchildren. "He'd tell us a little," said his older son, Steve. "But after awhile we just stopped asking him questions. He wanted to block it out. He never really wanted to talk about it. Even the medals and the Purple Heart he'd won but never received didn't seem to matter to him. They reminded him of what he wanted to forget, I guess."

What did matter was the journal, carefully kept for years. He had treasured it enough to bring it on the forced march to liberation in Braunau, Germany, a grueling sixteen-day expedition. He recorded his experiences even then, when every non-essential item was simply more weight to carry. Other men shed even their coats by the roadside, too tired to carry the extra weight, but Carano made sure his journal came home with him. After his death, the family took a renewed interest in the document, protecting its fragile, yellowing pages.

The story that follows is Steve Carano's own journal of survival, told in the writings and drawings created by him and his friends during their captivity in Stalag XVII B.

CLAUDIO "STEVE" CARANO'S
PRISONER OF WAR JOURNAL, STALAG 17

"A WARTIME LOG"

A REMEMBRANCE
FROM HOME
THROUGH THE AMERICAN Y.M.C.A.

PUBLISHED BY
THE WAR PRISONERS' AID OF THE Y.M.C.A.
37 QUAI WILSON
GENEVA—SWITZERLAND

This book belongs to Claudio S. Carano
2824 18th Street
Brooklyn, N.Y.

I am dedicating this book to my father, "Stefano Carano," who through all my life has tried, and I pray not in vain, to bring me up to be a good American. I am more than gratified for his untiring efforts, towards my two brothers and my wife. He has not failed to inspire in me the necessary common sense and the ability to face the hardships of life. Our family has suffered hardships and has also enjoyed the times of prosperity. I hope, through my love for him, and my family, he can always, for the remainder of his life, look upon us, and our accomplishments, as something of which to be proud. Without a doubt, he is the main factor in the upbringing and guidance of our lives.

Claudio "Steve" Carano
Prisoner of War
Krems, Austria 1944

In Memory of P. H.V. Sunde
D. C. McCutchen
L. Healy
Killed in Action
December 1, 1943

The Wire

"The Wire" is one of the most powerful pieces of writing in Carano's journal. Here, he conveys the mind-numbing boredom that led prisoners to count the thousands of barbs in the wire that confined them to Stalag XVII B. German guards were under orders to shoot to kill if a prisoner tried to cross the wire. Though a seemingly fragile boundary, that thread of barbed metal held the power of life and death: some despondent prisoners, wondering if the war would ever end, threw themselves at the wire in suicidal desperation, knowing that deadly shots would inevitably follow from the guard stations. Yet other prisoners found lessons in that fine line between captivity and freedom as they ruminated on the symbol that defined their lives. (Ironically, in his fantasies of faraway, exotic lands beyond incarceration, Carano refers to Baghdad as a romantic and dreamlike place, not the stuff of nightmares and chaos that it would become in yet another war.) Carano wrote "The Wire" on October 19, 1944—a month before he wrote his wife a letter outlining his plans to escape in November, an attempt that he never made.

The villain of these chronicles is "The Wire"—he is relentless, all powerful, omnipresent. He is the silent stern tyrant of all your days. "The Wire" is barbed, there are exactly 65,328 barbs in his stark perimeter. I have counted them. We all count them often! There used to be 65,329 barbs but lately one has rusted and fallen off. This was an event.

You can cheat "The Wire"—but not for long. Maybe for a day. Sometimes for two days in a row. You can turn your back to him and escape him by building a picture frame out of an old tin can or washing out your khaki trousers, or drawing a picture or scribbling a poem. But when you look back again, he is there. We have a dozen paths leading inward and away from him, but at day's end all paths lead back to him. "The Wire," he is always there, blocking every dream, every plan, every vain soaring of your enthusiasm. "The Wire" is at the end of every road, he is gaunt and he is cold, at dusk he frames the western sun in a black spider web of prickly steel. Even the sun is captive.

Some of us have been prisoners of war for eighteen months. Eighteen months is a year and a half, is seventy-two weeks, is five hundred and four days, is 12,096 hours, is 725,760 minutes. How long is a minute? A minute is a very long time. You can review your lifetime in a minute.

We come from every state in the Union. We come from the Air Corps, from the boundless blue sky. Maine and Washington are here. Boston and Birmingham, Providence and Pasadena. The gunners and paratroopers are here. We come from the fast wild whirl of front line aerial combat to an exile where the clock suddenly stops—and you could see time throbbing all around you like drowsy, never-ending heat waves.

We do not complain—that was long ago. Years ago, when we wore gray tweeds or blue serge, we used to complain, but not anymore. Elsewhere, there are many who are lying in muddy holes in the ground. There are some who look up at the rain, but do not feel the rain on their faces. Why should we complain? We are only in exile. We still have the sky and a dream.

Drab, khaki colored figures scuttle by in mud day in, day out. Only occasionally do you back up and take a romantic perspective on them as Americans and buddies. A year in a deep groove. The world is outside. We have only ourselves. The days do not contrast themselves. The only contrast is memory. One of the boys got a small phonograph from home. They were playing it in the barracks until all hours last night. I lay in my straw bed. It was very dark. I saw yesterday through the music. "Johnny Dough Boy Found a Rose"—"You are always in my heart"—"This love of mine." Old songs—old times. Then I was able to get a bird's eye view on this place. It is quite different when you step out of yourself and look down at yourself. You see a lot of strange things in the familiar.

You have a choice here: you can either be cynical and go to rot, or you can remember and still keep on hoping. I choose to remember. Some of my buddies search in the scrap heaps and keep making things. Some read. We endeavor to keep occupied. There is tomorrow. Tomorrow is a person —usually a lady—fair skin, scent, well-filled cheeks, laughter, permanence. "Going back" is another euphonic sound—like "jingle bells"—Remember? "Over there" is also very popular as a phrase. It means "tomorrow" and "going back." "Street car" has a nice sound too. Something like "Baghdad." "Aladdin" and other mysterious sounds of faraway lands.

Others of my buddies keep busy by taking meticulous care of their uniforms. Glossy shoes keep you remembering garrisons. It is good to remember garrisons. As for myself, I search the surrounding hills with thoughts and plans of home. While continuously walking the compound. You might call this sentiment. I do not apologize for it.

The best things of life are sentimental, patriotism, duty, love and little children. I see that very clearly now. Only a fool who is not taxed with actual reality dares assume that sentiment is unreal. You cease being a fad in a place like this. You are you!—There is no escaping it. Nowhere, and at no time, can a group of men live long together in isolation without giving birth to a tradition unique to the circumstances in which they are trapped. Hence we can and have become rather a species apart, with [a] distinctive logo, code, and—a set of hopes all our own. We have our code of honor, our code of morale, our code of responsibility, with the "American of tomorrow." We do not rust, we do a powerful lot of thinking.

Service life is fast. In training and on the line, a soldier is always three jumps ahead of his emotions, that is good. When you fly out deep into enemy territory and fate clips your wings beneath you—Captured—the days grow long, and there you sit and wait for all these emotions to catch up with you. They finally do, and that is not so good. Emotions are not military. They are embarrassing. When you get them you feel like a combat soldier with a rosebud in his breechlock. But if you ram the bolt home in disgust, you crush the flower all right, but then there is that damned cloying fragrance all around you. Most heartfelt sentiments or that particular one most dear, present themselves most often too late, making the feeling of them more hard to bear because their origin cannot be recalled.

Here in the absence of objective things we fall back upon the subjective. If a man's present is dead, then he has only the past, and the past is memory, and the memory is sentiment, how then, can a prisoner of war escape sentiment?

"Johnny O" is Army, every man's army. Johnny O is the composite soldier. He is all around one here in prison. He is likewise inside of me. He is cynic and lover, atheist and God, philosopher and clown. Sometimes he is very somber, at other times he is extremely lighthearted. It depends on the weather, the chow, mail from home, and the fortunes of war. To interpret him you must include his sentimentalism as well as his sophistication. The interest must be not as much in the literature of it as in honesty. . . .

"Johnny O" has not found himself as yet out of the many selves he has been, and must be in war. He will find himself. It is his determined effort. He keeps on looking. The important thing is that the gaze is upward.

And his chin is the same.

OCTOBER 19, 1944

P. O.W. KREMS, AUSTRIA

Holland

Carano wrote the following account of his capture by the Germans in Holland after he had been in Stalag XVII for several months. When the Red Cross distributed the blank, bound YMCA journals to prisoner of war camps, he used the first pages to write this narrative of the events leading up to his sixteen-month incarceration by the Germans.

November 30, 1943

We were briefed that morning for a mission to Leverkusen. We flew to within 20 miles of the enemy coast where the mission was scrubbed. I was flying with my own crew, so the scrub, after being awakened at 4:30 a.m., and going as far as we did, was sort of a disappointment. When we returned to the base, there was the usual clattering, mumbling, and arguments, among all the crews, including our own, as to whether we would be credited with a mission. That night "Blackie" [William Blackmon] and I, as was our daily routine, went to town, never for a moment thinking what fate might have had in store for us the following day, and days to come.

Forgotten Men

Folks remember and acclaim
the gunmen that still fly
We the prisoners are forgotten

though we once ruled the sky.
We too once forced the enemy
And challenged them to war,
Now that we have fallen,
They think of us no more.

DECEMBER 1, 1943

We were wakened that morning at 4:30 a.m., and of all the briefings we had, this was the first morning we had powdered, rather than fresh eggs for breakfast. The boys all went out to the ship to get their guns cleaned and ready for the trip, and I, being the "radio operator," went to the briefing room with the officers. I learned for the first time at briefing that Henslin, my pilot, was grounded and in the hospital, so naturally, I thought I wouldn't be flying that day. There was some confusion, as I was scheduled to fly as a spare radio operator, my name appeared on the board to fly with Malone and he, too, was grounded. Finally, they changed it again, and I was to fly with Flight Officer Sunde. Although I didn't know him, after a few words with him, I found him to be one of the finest men I'd met in the Army. We went out to the ship "097" together, where he introduced me to the crew. I didn't know any of these boys, as they were a new crew, like ours. By takeoff time, McCutchen and I were well acquainted, and I had some trouble with my gun, and he helped me get it ready before takeoff.

Takeoff was at 7:30 a.m. We assembled over England and after a while the group left the coast of England. Half way over the channel we thought we would have to abort. We couldn't get the flaps up. Josephson ("Joe") finally got them up with the hand crank, so we continued on with the others. We encountered our first flak over the Friesen Islands [in the North Sea].

When someone shouted over the Interphone "flak" at three o'clock, it was nothing to be alarmed about, as by this time, the danger of "flak" meant nothing at all to us. It just seemed like part of the sky that just had to be there. However, automatically, we put on our flak suits. I could see through the Radio Room door that the others were doing as I was. The flak that did come up was very little, and very inaccurate. This made me feel a lot more comfortable. It sort of took away the expectant feeling I had, since the moment I was told I would fly the mission as a spare radio operator on a strange crew.

In a short while we had a little excitement. "Fighters" came the word over the interphone, and several of them made a few passes at our formation, but from a distance. It gave the gunmen a chance to try a few pot shots at them. By this time we were well into enemy territory, and the going became a little rougher, as all eyes were straining to see some German fighter come in at us. There were several that flew far below the formation, dancing in and out of the clouds. Up to this time things were going fine, and it looked to us like this was going to be a "milk run," as all easy missions were so-called by combat crews. It was a very short time, after this feeling of safety, that we turned on our I.P. (Initial Point) and though we never felt the shock on lift of the ship, as it hit, number three engine was hit by flak. To the astonishment of the crew, Sunde yelled the order, "Prepare to bail out!"

In a few seconds, we didn't quite grasp the meaning of those words. Joe (Josephson) was the first to act, being nearest the waist door. By the time myself and the others were rid of our flak suits, he had the door out, and in a kneeling position, waited for the order to go. In removing my flak suit, I was lucky enough not to tear the wire loop from my headset. So I heard the order, "Back to stations, we'll try to make it back to England."

I yelled over the interphone for anyone to hear, to "Stop Joe," stop him before he falls out. But in the excitement I wasn't heard. Culver, who also wore one interphone, evidently heard the same order, grabbed Joe and yanked him back, just as he was about to fall out from lack of oxygen. Culver had him back on oxygen and in a few moments he was all right, and back at his gun. In the meantime, Culver went back to the tail and, after some trouble with him, managed to get Johnnie back on oxygen. Johnnie was almost out and insisted on putting the mask on himself and couldn't.

In coming out of the ball-turret, McCutchen, while trying to get his parachute on, passed out from lack of oxygen. I put his mask on him again, and in a few moments he was all right. By this time, we had flown away from the formation losing altitude, when three German fighters attacked us. All except McCutchen were already back at our guns.

In the chase that followed, Sunde flew that B-17 in such a way as to make any pursuit pilot turn green with envy. We were thrown around in the ship like a pair of dice would be in a glass. One of the Huns in his first pass got Joe pretty bad on the left waist gun; a 20 m.m. shattered the gun and Joe's arm and hand, like so many match sticks, rendering both helpless. At about the same time Sunde dove the ship straight for the cover of clouds. I might add, at this point in my story, that safe and comfortable feeling I had a short while ago, was now gone.

Under cover of cloud we had a short breathing spell, and we needed it. The inside of our ship looked as though a cyclone had hit it, parachute bags were strewn about everywhere, ammunition boxes and belts were all over the ship, the odor of burnt powder and flesh prevailed in every corner of the ship, and it was sickening. It was during this breathless spell that I prayed. It seemed I said a thousand prayers over and over again.

Calling to Sunde, as I would my own pilot Lieutenant Henslin, I asked, "How we doin' boss? We gonna make it?"

"Sure," was the reply. "With a little luck."

With this assurance, I went back to the waist to see if there was anything that could be done. Seeing that both Josephson and McCutchen were badly hit, I started to wipe Mac's face free of the blood that was trickling down, but he shook me off saying he was all right. So turning to Joe, and using my lady leg knife [a folding pocket knife with a sheath shaped like a woman's leg] that I always carried with me, started to hack away the sleeve on Joe's left arm. After what seemed like hours, I had him patched up neatly (like a pillow tied with a piece of string), but under the circumstances it was the best I could do.

About this time, the enveloping clouds that were hiding us gave out, and above the thundering noise and vibration that seemed to threaten to break our eardrums, we heard a peculiar sound. It sounded like a child running a stick along a corrugated tin building. It was strange to me, as this was the first experience we had of flak hitting the ship. We all were huddled together in the waist when this started. Upon looking out the window to my surprise, I saw that we were flying about five thousand feet above a city.

Sunde called and told us it was probably the City of Cologne and we were going to "hit the deck." Those gunners who were now shooting at us were pretty good. It seemed they never missed a shot, as holes appeared in all parts of the ship, like spots before a drunkard's eyes. As we left the outskirts of the city, it seemed that only a miracle kept the ship in the air. The co-pilot, Sweeney, who also was flying this trip as a spare, came back to the waist to see how things were going. If I could put into writing the expression on his face as he stared into the waist from the radio room door, my story could end right here. What he saw was a B-17 generally in tip top order and spic and span, turned into a horrible confusion of blood, and debris. Everyone in the waist had been hit by flak over Cologne.

McCutchen, who had been hit before, was even worse now, but he still insisted he was "all right." We called to Johnnie in the tail and the first thing we heard was a stream of curse words. We asked him if he was hit and did he need any help, but he said he was just nicked in the leg, and it was nothing, then he went on with his cursing. I had some cigarettes and lit one for Joe, Mac, and myself. We were all hit bad, but the feelings amongst us were high as several times we called up to both pilot and navigator, "Boys, we gonna make it? Where are we at, Chris?" the answers were, as before, "Sure we'll make it," and from Chris, "We'll be over Holland in a few minutes." Looking out the windows we were flying so low, it seemed we braced ourselves a thousand times for the crash that didn't come.

We were spurred into action again as Chris, I believe it was, shouted over the interphone, "Fighters!" Seeing that Joe could not handle his gun, I started to charge it. I tugged and tugged at the damned charging handle, I even put my foot up to it, but the damned thing wouldn't budge. In the excitement of the second danger of fighters, I had completely forgotten Joe's gun had been smashed.

As I darted for my own gun in the radio room, I saw McCutchen on the right waist gun blazing away at a fighter coming at us at 5 o'clock. Going to the radio room, I found I couldn't use my left foot properly. It felt as though it was broken at the ankle. When I did get to my gun, I was mad as hell, as the fighters were attacking us from the sides and front, and my gun had only a small area above, and to the rear, in which I could fire. These fighters must have known after the first few passes, that most of our guns were out, as they came to within 25 to 50 feet away from us before they would pull away.

I saw the plane go down in smoke at about 5 o'clock, and thought it was either Hap in the top turret or Johnnie in the tail that got him. But after looking back at the tail I knew immediately that it must have been Hap that got the fighter. All that was left of the tail was just a skeleton in shreds. Johnnie must surely have been dead. I don't even try to recall how long this attack lasted, but presently the fighters that did remain either ran out of gas or were called back, for they left us.

Here again we had another breather. I have tried to describe what the inside of the ship looked like before this last attack. It would be impossible to describe it now, with photographs. From here on out, we thought it best to stay at our positions. Sweeney called and asked how we were. We told him that the only gun in the rear in working order was my radio room gun, and that isn't of very much use when attacked from the front, or sides of the ship. We had no chance to check on Johnnie in the tail, but from the condition of the tail, as I've said before, he must surely have been dead.

We were flying so low this time, on several occasions we passed houses and windmills where we could actually see clear through the windows in the front and rear of them. Once we passed over some kind of field, or infantry camp, and a German guard on its outskirts was shooting at us with his rifle. Luckily, no one was hit by him.

At this time we learned that Sunde was hit pretty bad in the last attack, and although Sweeney, the Co-Pilot, took over the controls, Sunde, though wounded badly from a 20 M.M. that exploded at his side, still managed to help Sweeney fly the ship. We were now in a bad state, but miraculously still flying. Almost all of the control cables were shot away and strewn all over the waist, [the] number three engine was still windmilling, threatening to shake the right wing loose. Number one engine was leaking gas, yet Sunde still said over the interphone, "We'll make it."

I asked Chris once again, where we were at. He replied, "About five minutes from the coast." When we heard that, we surely thought we would make it.

Then the dirty bastards attacked us again. And they must have been told that we evidently had no guns in use, as they threw all caution to the winds, coming in very close for the kill. It was during this last attack, that thoughts raced through my mind such as, in the next few minutes, there would be ten dead men who almost made it back to England.

I prayed, with my eyes straining to catch one of them within range of my gun, yet praying hard and fast as though I wouldn't have time to finish. Suddenly I felt a hot stinging feeling in my right foot. The panel door to the bomb-bay splintered behind me. Then I saw the cause for it, an ME-109 came up as if out of the ground at our tail. It seemed so close, I thought it would ram us. I can't explain what it was that spurred me. I felt as though I couldn't move a muscle. Squeezing the trigger I saw pieces of his plane tear loose.

Suddenly my gun stopped firing, why I didn't know, until I looked down and saw that my hand and the handle of the gun had been smashed. By this time the 109 had disappeared. All this, which though it may sound like hours, must actually have taken place in a few seconds. Scared—scared wasn't the word for it—petrified shitless would be more appropriate. After what seemed like ages I started for a belt of ammunition lying across the ball-turret. As I bent down to pick it up, the ship lurched upwards pinning me to the floor. It was then my left hand was hit and a bullet tore through the rest of my heavy flying suit. While trying to get the ammunition belt into the gun, the crash came.

There was no warning, no expecting it, no nothing, just an impact that pinned me to the bulkhead, a terribly loud noise, two lurches, then silence. The water was about knee-high before I realized that we had crashed. Strangely enough at this instant, I was no longer scared or in a hurry. It just seemed as though I had been expecting it and this was the end of the line. Starting out the escape hatch of the radio room, I had a glimpse of the waist. It was half-full of water, and down beside the ball turret I saw Joe. I couldn't see his body, just his side of the ship and with every once of strength I had, I gave a final heave.

It could only have been the "will of God," that I should live. Upon reaching the surface I thought my lungs would break with all the air and water I sucked in. It took me a few seconds before I could think clearly. About fifteen feet away I could see several of the others in the dinghy. I called for help but it was just a whisper. I don't recall exactly how I made it to the raft. One moment I would be up, the next under. It must have been the tide and what little swimming I could manage with all my flying clothes on, including the fur lined boots. Chris and Joe grabbed me by the collar, then "Chris" put his arm around my neck and held my head above water. Joe was in the raft, paddling, and every time he'd lean forward, his knee, which was on the edge of the raft, would press down on my head. I was too far gone to even tell him to stop.

Two Dutchmen came out in a rowboat and I could hear Chris yelling for them to get me in quickly. Lying on the floor of the boat, I had my first chance to really think, though I couldn't move even a finger. My mind was surprisingly clear. I said a prayer and thanked God for sparing me. As we neared the shore there were hundreds of people lined along the dike. Someone brought a ladder which served as a stretcher to carry me to the house. Four of the others were already there lying on the floor, where the Dutch had spread hay.

At first no one could speak. Cold and hurt as we were, everyone had the same thought in mind. Here were only five of us in the room, yet there were ten in the ship when it hit the water. Joe and Sweeney were brought to the room that we were in, accompanied by a German guard. This was our first view of a German soldier. And what a rough looking character: he seemed to us like a comic strip character in a movie. It was Joe who told us that we seven were the only ones to get out of the ship. Sunde, McCutchen and Healy did not. Three of the nicest, bravest men I have had the occasion to meet, and fight with in combat, were dead. Seven men in a single room and dozens of Dutch people trying to crowd in, every one of them eager to help. Some brought us food, drinks of all kinds, and dry underwear.

When they finally brought a civilian doctor, he did the best he could to stop the bleeding of six men who were just pouring blood. All he had with him were some bandages and powder. Joe never did get any bandages as there were none left. A Dutch woman gave him a towel to wipe the blood. After a few minutes the towel looked like a piece of red flannel underwear. He and Sweeney were the lucky ones that day, they both had a suit of Dutch clothes to wear. (If their wives ever saw them, in those zoot suits, they'd divorce them.) We laughed and mimicked the Germans so much about these suits the Dutch honestly thought we were mad.

There is one person in Holland we will never forget. He could speak very good English. He made the mistake of asking if any of us would like a cup of coffee. Anyone that knows me well knows that this was a mistake. I believe that day I came closer to drowning from coffee than I did in the water. It was so cold, for a while we thought we lived the last few hours only to freeze to death on this straw-covered floor.

Towards evening an ambulance arrived to take us to a hospital. That ride in itself was an ordeal. Hap had a 20 MM hole in his ankle and it was hanging limp over the edge of the stretcher. The dirty German bastard who was driving never missed a bump. Although we asked him several times to slow down he never paid any attention to us, instead he drove faster. He seemed to enjoy hurting us. We arrived about one hour later at St. Mary's hospital in Khoda, Holland, which was under the supervision of nuns who were very quick, efficient, and pleasant with us. It was at this hospital that we received our first good medical treatment, after patching us good and proper with yards and yards of paper bandage, we were placed in prison ward, two in a room. Tully and I were together. He had some flak in his back and spent a terrible night with it.

The following morning, December 2, we were moved to the Luftwaffe Hospital in Holland. This hospital was used for German airmen, being one of the biggest and best in Holland. The trip to Amsterdam was just a reciprocal of the day before. On our way we passed through "Chips," Holland's "La Guardia field." It didn't take a second look to see that our boys had visited "Chips" frequently. The hangars were just giant skeletons, black and smudgy. Debris was scattered everywhere. Where we arrived at the lazarette we were immediately attended to. Casts, stitches, bandages, etc.

The doctors and nurses were German; though they were very good at their work they still regarded us as enemies, and showed it. Two of the nurses really were swell to us. The others, well, they were Germans. One of these had a husband who was a prisoner of war in the States. We'd get her mad as hell saying when the war ends he won't want to leave the U.S. and she would have to go to him, rather than vice versa. The other one, Charlotte, was the doctor's right hand chick who attended all our bandaging. Maybe it was because they were the only pretty things around us that we thought they were swell to us; at any rate, we did think so.

"Rufus," as we so nicknamed Bernard Van Haben (sounds like a German diplomat) was our room orderly. Between the three of them trying to learn to speak English, and we trying the opposite, you can imagine what went on in that single room. They would try to prove to us that we were "Luftgangsters" and we men there proved the contrary. In fact, after a few weeks that we were there, Ottie was ready to pack her bag and leave for the good old U.S.A.

I believe the German people are a very foolish race. Half of them don't know what they are fighting for; the other half are the Nazi fanatics that should be exterminated. Why, they were astounded to hear of the luxuries that existed in the United States even during wartime. These included high-ranking officers as well as the privates and civilians. For instance, the food. We complained so about the quality and minimum amount we were served. They stood open mouthed in awe at the tales we told them of our American dinner (slightly exaggerated). While in the hospital this was our daily menu: Breakfast: two slices of "brot," a German substitute for bread, made of wood pulp. Dinner, this was a feast. "Kartoffeln mit fleisch"— boiled spuds and horsemeat. Twice a week they would add about eight pounds of cabbage to it, red cabbage at that. Supper was a treat, two slices of "brot mit balony" und kaffee. This "kaffee" was some liquid concoction they called coffee.

A week before Christmas, we received our English prisoner of war parcel and one more on Christmas Eve. The Germans, who had been drooling at the mouth by this time, almost went nuts when Hap piled the contents of his two parcels beside him, the way a grocer displays his merchandise in a window. He was politely asked to put it back in the boxes. "Rufus," who was to leave New Year's Day for a sixteen-day fur-lough with his family in Munster, couldn't resist asking us for a package of tea to take home to his wife, who loved a cup of tea and hadn't had any in the past five years. Each of us offered him a package. When he saw how little we valued this great luxury, tears came into his eyes. He never again called us "Luft gangsters." We later learned tea in the German black market was valued at one hundred dollars a pound.

DECEMBER 31, 1943

On New Year's Eve, we were moved to Dulag Luft, a German inter-rogation center. [This is probably the center at Wetzlar, Germany.] The dirty bastards stole all our flying clothes. We told them they came to the hospital with us on top of the ambulance. They said we never had any with us. We were given a pair of Dutch civilian pants and underwear apiece. And with this excess amount of clothing we left the hospital walk-ing barefoot in snow. After being in a warm room for one month, I don't have to mention how cold we were.

They drove us to the station in Amsterdam by ambulance, where we boarded a hospital car (with no heat) in which we had to ride all day, with other Americans that we picked up along the way, to Dulag Luft.

This trip to Germany was something we will never forget. Going through Holland was a pretty sight, beautiful homes, windmills, dikes, etc. You'd never know there was a war going on all around it. The scars of war were evident from the moment we crossed the German border. Here we saw what we never could see from the air. Some folks will never know what a bombed city looks like, and I hope our folks in the U.S. never do, not even in pictures.

We have seen bombed cities, many of them on our trip through Germany, proper. Cologne and Dusseldorf are only two of the larger cities, not to mention dozens of smaller cities and towns that were completely destroyed. We lay over in Cologne for a few hours. Here was a city leveled to debris and ashes. The Cathedral of Cologne, which stood about fifty yards from the station, was a pitiful sight, once a proud beautiful building, where once hundreds of people went to worship, was now just another torn victim of Allied bombings.

People stared at us some with contempt, others with pity, all of them wondering why we were here. As I've said before, the German propaganda machine, which in reality is even more powerful than Adolf Hitler, branded us "Luft Gangsters," so these poor simple-minded people stared, or thought they were staring, at "Luft Gangsters" who flew all the way from Chicago to Germany just to bomb their homes. Not one of them knew what a gangster was.

We arrived at Stalag XVII B on the morning of January eighth. The camp was three miles from Krems in Austria, and all those who were wounded and couldn't walk were taken by truck, including myself.

Before mingling with the other American prisoners, we were deloused. This included having all our hair cut off, and our clothing placed in cyanide ovens for six hours. While waiting for our clothes to come out, we almost froze as we stood nude for six hours in a concrete room which had no heat at all.

Culver and Joe went directly to the barracks after delousing but before I finally joined them, I spend one week in the "Revier" because of my injured hand and foot. There was no room for us new prisoners so we had to double up with the older "Kriegies." In most cases we were sleeping three in a bed, but it certainly was a relief after a month and a half to be amongst a bunch of Americans, regardless of the conditions.

The first few weeks were quite eventful, meeting old buddies shot down before and after we were, some of whom we even believed dead.

From the very beginning, Culver and I went into combine, and a better combine partner I couldn't find out of the 4,500 men in camp, with the exception of Joe who was in another barrack. Sleeping in the adjoining bunk was Charlie Groth of Brooklyn. Charlie is another friend who's tops with me in camp, even though we two hard-heads can't agree one little bit in an argument.

I had searched this camp every day for weeks hoping to find someone from my base who was shot down after I was, for information about Andy, Blackie, or anyone else in my own crew. They all seemed to know Blackie, saying he was okay. But no one seemed to know about Andy.

The winter here was intolerable, mud which came up over our ankles after every little rain. Cold! I never thought a place could be so cold. There are not many people who will believe this but it's true. Last winter we slept with every bit of clothing we could possibly get hold of, besides the two skimpy blankets the Germans issued us. Many was the day we stayed in bed all day long, trying to keep a little warm.

The food was another problem, which was unbearable. We received one butter can full of soup which was nothing but the water used to boil carrots. We were also given a small ration of wood pulp bread and hot water in the mornings. If it wasn't for the Red Cross parcels we receive each Friday, half of us would have gone mad, the other half would have starved to death. This is actually true, as we see proof of it every day when a dead Russian or Italian goes by on a stretcher.

Life in the Prison Camp

The Geneva Convention, expanded in 1929 by cooperating nations, ensured that prisoners of war would receive medical care and subsistence rations from captors. Both the United States and Germany had signed the convention, ensuring certain basic humane conditions for their own soldiers. Stalin's disregard for the convention guaranteed that Russian prisoners received brutal treatment and, through the wire separating Russians from Americans, Carano witnessed firsthand the starvation and bitter cold that the brave Russians endured. He offered his painful observations of both Russian and Italian prisoners of war, and the relative privileges of the French, who at least received decent burials.

Russian and Italian prisoners are kept in the compound adjoining ours. Theirs is a pitiful wretched existence. Whenever we get the chance we would throw them pieces of bread or a cigarette, they would half kill each other trying to get it. We had snow for sixty-one consecutive days, and the Russian and Italian prisoners were forced to work in it without coats or decent shoes.

The French prisoners were better treated than any others, receiving close to a brotherly affection. From France, they received personal parcels of food, clothing, tobacco, and mail. Although forced in return to work, they received many privileges denied all other nationalities. From the countryside while on "commando work," they were able to obtain nearly all the luxuries the Germans themselves were given. For good behavior they were given furloughs of several weeks to return to France to visit their families. These were freely granted and no guard accompanied them. If an extension of these furloughs were requested, two or more Frenchmen had to return to Germany to work in the prisoner's absence. The numbers varied depending on the prisoner's rank and occupation. French funerals were conducted with all military honors as prescribed by France.

Carano copied a letter into his journal written by a French major named Clayeux to Kenneth "Kurt" Kurtenbach, Stalag XVII's "Man of Confidence," who was elected to that office by the his comrades to negotiate between them and their German captors. Clayeux, the commanding officer of wounded French prisoners within the German camp, praises the American POWs for their show of respect when the French buried a dead officer.

From: Major Clayeux
            Senior officer of French prisoners hospitalized in
            Gniexeldorf Lazarett
To: S/SGT Kurtenbach

My dear comrade—

The officers of the delegation who accompanied the burial party of Captain Broque to the Stalag cemetery were deeply touched, as they passed your camp, by the correct military attitude by all the American prisoners, when the coffin with the French Flag passed before them.

It seemed to us on this occasion that over and beyond the respect shown the dead, there manifested itself across the barbed wire which separates us, a mutual understanding, an intimate communion in the same faith.

In the name of the French Officer, prisoners who felt the fervor of this spontaneous gesture beg to you to transmit to your comrades the homages of our ardent friendship.

MAJOR CLAYEUX
Senior Officer of French prisoners
in Krems, Austria

The Poles, Serbs, Greeks, and Yugoslavs had similar treatment to the French, with the exception of furloughs, and many strict limitations.

The Italians were looked upon with contempt by all nationalities, including the Germans. This was due to Italy's conduct during the War. Many stories have been told us, most of them from our own American boys who were shot down and captured in Italy, of the underhanded treachery, cowardice, cruelty, and arrogance of the Italians towards the captured Americans and others. To the Italian soldier who received no aid through the International Red Cross or home, the Germans were especially cruel. Examples of cruelty were many. One morning an Italian soldier was killed for no reason at all. His offense was catching cigarettes thrown over the fence to him by an American boy. He was shot through the neck and left to die while the guard walked on by him, continuing his tour. Many was the time they were forced outdoors in weather twenty degrees below zero. In fact, whenever it struck some German officer's fancy, which was very often.

The American soldier is always ready to lend an ear or a consoling word to anyone. With the Italian he had few, if any sympathetic words. Cases of brutal treatment at his hand were still very fresh in the minds of most American airmen captured in Italy. Of all [the] inhuman treatment of prisoners of war, the Italian nation was among the worst. Such stories of American prisoners of war in Italy having to barter with personal property and jewelry for a drink of water, which the Italian guards in prison camps had shut off for days at a time, were common. Men weak from starvation were confined close to Italian kitchens where the aromas of cooking food were ever at hand. Our contact with them as fellow prisoners here in camp was not by any means pleasant. In trying to gain favor with the Germans, they would resort to anything, from stealing from their fellow prisoners to reporting to the Germans any attempt at escape they may have overheard while working in the American or French compounds. From the Italians who were without honor, personal or national pride, little could be expected. One German guard could be reasonably sure of obedience even from large numbers of them. The poor Italian was almost a man without a country, depending solely on the Germans for his food, clothing, and hospital care. Funerals for Italian officers were performed with some military honors, while the enlisted men were wrapped in ordinary brown paper and buried in a hole without even a plain wooden box.

The Germans' fear and hatred for the Russian is beyond imagination. The Russian government's refusal to sign with the Geneva Convention gave the Germans free minds to devise all the atrocities imaginable. Many of these inhuman outrages proved fatal to hundreds of Russians. Receiving no aid from Russia or the International Red Cross, the poorly fed and poorly clothed Russians lived like caged animals. Several times each week we received word from them, pleading and begging for aid from the Americans which the Germans would not allow, although daily we would dump vast amounts of German soup which our stomachs were not strong enough to consume. This waste, poor though it was, would certainly have saved hundreds of Russians from starvation, as there were approximately two Americans to every Russian in camp. On their starvation rations, they were driven to the limit of their ability to produce for the German war machine.

In every city, town, and village in German-controlled Europe, Russian slaves were used to do dirty hard work. Russian men, women, and children from conquered territories were brought to Germany by the train-loads. Upon arriving, they were taken to delousing station, stripped regardless of sex in prison yards awaiting their clothes to be steamed and gassed. They were inspected naked for fleas and lice by German guards regardless of weather conditions. To be beaten, cursed, have dogs turned on them, to be naked in the cold, rain, or snow and punished with imprisonment or death for the slightest display of revolt, was all the Russian could expect at the hands of his German conquerors.

During the winter and spring, on their poor food, with no heat in overcrowded barracks, they died by the dozens. Funerals were an insult to the Christian world. To conserve space and clothing, they were stripped naked, wrapped in brown wrapping paper and buried in a hole four or five at a time. In my opinion, the Russian is a fearless soldier who will never knuckle down to the German. In fact, in some cases, we have seen here in camp, it was the German who knuckled down.

The German people feared and hated the American flying personnel, still they held admiration for them simply because they were Americans. Tales of hangings, shootings, beatings, and firings were witnessed and experienced by many that were unfortunate enough to be shot down over German cities. The ability of the German Army to capture disabled fliers quickly saved untold numbers of men. The Germans' attitudes toward

Americans differed as the seasons of the year. One day, a friendly cooperative spirit, the next a cold and arrogant one. They spared little to keep us confined, a double barbed wire fence ten feet high with entanglements in between them. Control towers at every vulnerable spot, equipped with searchlights and machine guns. A warning wire marked a forbidden area twenty feet from the inside fence, with walking guards, outpost guards with dogs and strongly defended gates.

The food ration, though better than any other nationality received, was terrible. The soup was made of carrots or rutabagas and salted water to which occasionally was added a small portion of rotten moldy horsemeat. Mashed winter stored potatoes and corned beef from our Red Cross parcels was a delicacy. Saturday and Sunday mornings we received cooked prunes which were also from our parcels. Every other morning we received hot water alone. When potatoes were plentiful we received them daily for weeks—likewise with carrots or rutabagas. Our German meals (all three of them) depended on a plentiful season. The cooking was done in a large kitchen and carried to the barracks in wooden tubs.

The lack of hospitals, an institution taken for granted in America, lost the life, limbs and health of untold hundreds of boys that would only have been laid up a short while given proper care. Bandages, medicines, doctors, etc., were often denied or unobtainable. Wounds were dressed not more than once every ten days, even in the larger hospitals. Because of [their] good physical condition, many recovered that otherwise would have succumbed to the many wound infections.

On occasion, the precious Red Cross boxes delivered sports equipment gathered for the American soldiers by the YMCA. This was a luxury unheard of in the Russian or Italian camps. To pass the time, the men boxed or watched a comrade such as Joe Hafer, once a professional boxer, demonstrate his skills in the ring.

Our boxing ring was made entirely of salvaged odds and ends, with a mound of dirt for a floor. The gloves were furnished by the Red Cross.

Volleyball and basketball were very popular, nets, balls and baskets furnished by Red Cross, played on dirt floor.

Though the men had access to exercise equipment and a playing field and were given subsistence rations, Carano's journal makes it clear that life in Stalag XVII was a dehumanizing experience, subject to the vagaries and whims of the German guards. Carano and his comrades understood that only the agreements of the Geneva Convention allowed them to survive during incarceration.

Maltreatment, though not quite as severe as in cases of other nationalities, nevertheless was on a level with the treatment of criminals and animals. Forced to stand for hours in snow during a personal search or roll call, restrictions of privileges, delousings and threats of imprisonment were the usual outbursts of German temper. One case of murder in Stalag XVII will stand as a symbol of Nazi oppression in the minds of the American boys intered there.

On the evening of December 3, 1943, while trying to escape, one boy was killed and two were wounded sleeping in the barracks into which the Germans had fired. The Germans would not turn on the lights and the two wounded boys were operated on by the mediocre light of butter-burners by the American surgical officer.

In spite of all the hardships the American spirits in us never died. Little did we realize how truly great America really is while we were flying. Yet it took but a short while from the time we were shot down until the first month after we arrived at XVII to realize who and what we fought for.

To the American International Red Cross and the Geneva Convention the lives of all of us here in XVII B are indebted. We can never repay the Red Cross adequately for their parcels of food, clothing, and medical and sports equipment, etc. And for the Geneva Convention, which protected us against the atrocities inflicted upon other nationalities. For their help we give thanks. And to the mothers and fathers who brought us up to be true Americans all we can say is thank God we are Americans.

Jerry Warning

During his long months of captivity in Stalag XVII, Carano was able to recall the details of his capture in great specificity, perhaps remembered in the boredom and loneliness of time spent in his bunker. This anecdote is a telling window into the mind of the German captors.

Although this certain incident took place more than ten months ago, I can still recall some of the words a German officer made when I was leaving Frankfurt, Germany for this camp here at Krems, Austria. He said, "Remember gentlemen, we are German, we are warriors. We were born to fight and we are not afraid to die. I have given strict orders to my men: they will not hesitate to shoot you if you do not obey my orders. These soldiers, German soldiers, have my orders to kill you, you will not get away. You gentlemen are soldiers, and your country will be judged by your actions, so behave gentlemen, behave! Do not try to escape."

Escape Letter to Rose

In the late autumn of 1944, Steve Carano decided to make an escape attempt with two of his comrades, despite such Nazi warnings as the admonition to "behave or be shot." Below is a secret letter he wrote to his wife Rose, and then entrusted to his buddy and fellow Brooklynite Charles Groth for safe keeping. His plans to escape never came to fruition.

NOVEMBER 19, 1944

Darling,

This letter may never reach you, for no one knows what the outcome of this war will be, or what may befall the bearer, as I am entrusting it to a very dear friend, who I am sure will do his utmost to deliver it. His name is Charles Groth, and if anything should happen to me, I know he can tell you and you would like to know about myself and the way we have lived in this hole. In this way only can you know why I and Josephson and Bang are attempting this escape. One year in a German prison camp is just one year too long to be away from the ones I love, especially yourself and my son who is growing rapidly and forgetting (if ever he knew) that his father really existed. Something just has to be done and, as you my wife know, how long I can possibly be tied down in one place, especially being away from you, Stevie, Mom and Dad.

I somehow feel that if I didn't at least try to get home before these damned Germans decide to quit, I don't feel that I could ever again feel as though I was half the man I ever considered myself. If anything should happen to me and my two buddies, I want you to know that it is for the love of the ones at home that we are trying our best to go to them as quickly as possible.

I ALWAYS HAVE AND ALWAYS WILL LOVE YOU ALL,

STEVE

Six Months a Prisoner of War

Carano's essay, "Six Months a Prisoner of War," allows glimpses into how the young men survived psychologically through memories of home, a sense of humor, camaraderie, the power of the imagination, and the knowledge that they were suffering for a worthy cause.

The first few months of prison life with all early difficulties to adjustment of capture [was] an existence with many hard and trying days, and strange to say, many amusing ones. It is hard to explain the changes in a man's life from great freedom, none more than flying to one of bondage. There are many that we have to accustom ourselves with that are in many ways, more wrecking mentally and physically than combat. With the many hours of inactivity there is left a great deal of time for thoughts to come to mind. Many past days of endless enjoyments are called to remembrance in the face of dull lengthy hours. The little things of an American way of life most assuredly come, most every day, [and] can be heard from prisoners reminiscing. "Man, I wonder what white bread tastes like" and "I'd like to see a good movie"—thoughts that are in the mind of every P. O. W.—thoughts that hurt a bit and must be steeled against.

Wondering how the folks at home are getting along and longing to see them again. A pining memory of things missed, a great thrill at things once enjoyed. An empty stomach makes a man see the truer things of life.

There were a couple of weeks during the winter that there were no Red Cross parcels in camp. We lived on carrots and water soup and relished it. A man's mind becomes stuck on one thought—food. It could be seen on all the faces. I was one of them. We tried to catch snow birds with box traps, and lived in hopes that the Jerries would send their boys into the barracks. What gigantic feasts can be conjured by the mind when a mind is hungry. The bitter cold made matters worse and to top the situation, the people back home were being led to believe that we were being treated well and led a life at least with good quarters, food and entertainment. What hurt us all more than all the discomforts and hardships that we had to go through, to starve, to suffer, to live in dire filthiness, all well and good, these a soldier can face and undergo for his country and people, but if there is not an understanding of this sacrifice, his spirit suffers greatly.

But thoughts seldom linger long for discussion. We have learned to fight the mental battle, too. It is rightly put to say in the least, that the Germans are in many ways amazed with Americans, especially by their spirit. How we manage to laugh and sing, as if being a prisoner, living as we do, is only a bad odor to be put up with until the coming tides wash it away.

The Story of Slim Lassiter

"Slim" Lassiter, an imposing, quiet soldier from Chicago who stood six feet seven inches tall, impressed Carano with his steely resolve and fortitude. When Lassiter finally told his story of capture and his near-escape from the Germans in France, Carano wrote it down meticulously, careful to get every detail of his extraordinary story correct. Storytelling, about either capture or near-escapes, offered both a way of passing the time and of establishing bonds among the men. As a precaution against giving the Germans valuable information, Carano carefully omitted the names of Lassiter's comrades, drawing a blank line instead. Throughout this segment, the blank lines refer to Lassiter's pilot, first engineer, copilot, and ball turret gunner, who accompanied him throughout the ordeal, as well as the French who helped them.

NOT WITHOUT HONOR
ST. MATTHEW XIII—57

There is one aspect of life as a prisoner of war which many of us did not experience. The following is one amongst hundreds of similar incidents that have happened to American airmen. This particular one is that of escape and capture: a story of the attempt made to get back to England after the forced landing made in France.

It is written exactly as related to me by one of the members of the crew, T/SGT Joe E. "Slim" Lassiter, Radio Operator on one of the bombers that made perilous flights over enemy territory, never to return. It is difficult and beyond my capacity for description to perhaps write it down as it should be written for others to understand. However, the truth and facts need little description—to these I did confine this writing. Some things are beyond the reach of descriptive words. To understand the feeling of the starved, one must have experienced hunger to the extent of starvation. For many who may read this there will follow little actual understanding and some of the minor points most probably will be taken lightly—as of little consequence or importance.

A drowning man will clutch madly at a straw.

Lassiter is a man gigantic in stature who towers above all men not only because of his height but also by his quiet understanding—piercing eyes that see much but show little, a silence of manner that commands respect without force. Perhaps the quietest man I have ever met. When forced to speak it is with a slow drawl, spaced with clear thinking and a great deal of modesty. I am quite sure there are marks left upon his inner self by this experience alone that perhaps no one will ever know.

It all began with his last bombing mission to St. Nazaire, France, on May 24th, 1943. Their ship was attacked by the still mighty German Luftwaffe. From both the fighters and the flak they caught hell. With two engines burning their ship was sent toward earth with a blazing inferno. Slim was hit in the hand. All of the crew were trying desperately to bail out. One by one they left the ship which was by this time diving and climbing at a terrific speed out of control. Slim looked about for this seat-type parachute. It wasn't in its place, the engineer, amidst all the confusion of ammunition boxes flying about, equipment smashing here and there, had taken Slim's chute by mistake. The fights were by this time in for the kill, pouring their 20 MM through the crippled plane. Slim found a chute and made a mad try to get it on but with a badly mangled hand it was utterly hopeless. Looking up in desperation he saw the ball turret gunman leave the plane just as the stabilizer hit the tree-tops. The ship miraculously bellied in and settled. Slim and the pilot scrambled out just as a German fighter came swooping from overhead.

Slim dived under the ship. After the passing attack Slim came out. The Pilot, ———, was in near hysterics from the terrific strain of landing the ship. They both went through the ship to make sure no other members of the crew were left aboard. Finding no one else there, they started to leave the plane, but soon turned and decided to go back and set fire to the plane to prevent the Germans from finding any useful material or information. Slim re-entered the ship, found the pilot's automatic, with which they fired into the gasoline tank and ignited the leaking fuel. It went up in a roar of flame and smoke. Taking off his "Mae West" [a life preserver that, when inflated, gave its wearer a bosom effect] and flying equipment, Slim threw them into the fire. As the two flyers turned to leave, they saw surrounding them some fifty Frenchmen seemingly directed into three groups, each one wanting ———— and Slim to follow them. They decided to cast their lot with one of the groups and followed them. They were taken down the hill to a peasant farmhouse where they were billeted in the loft of the barn adjoining the house.

The French brought some civilian clothes and shoes, a pair of canvas slippers for Slim: the only thing they could get to fit his size 12 feet. Butter, bread, and cider were also given them. Shortly afterward, however, no sooner than Slim and his comrade had rested a bit, the French came running to them screaming, "Partier!" "Partier! Allemagne!" (Meaning, go quickly—the Germans are near).

They immediately left, accompanied by the French[man] who also took them over many fields and fences before they halted at one corner of the field where they sat down to rest again and eat. There, they remained until dark (10:30 p.m.). At this time they were taken by an old Frenchman across the highway and told their direction for travel. He left them then, as he wanted no more to do with helping them escape, as it was too dangerous. Slim and ———— walked along the highway for nearly a mile before they crossed a fence and lay down to sleep. This was impossible as it was too cold. They huddled together as close as possible to keep warm. Slim's hand had now begun to give him much pain. At dawn they awoke and continued walking some ten miles towards Pontevie, France. They kept to the road despite the frequent meetings with German soldiers walking toward them. However, this bold attitude proved their best cover. The Germans started but did not stop or question them. They walked on and circled the town. Nearing a house, ———— went forward to ask for help while Slim lay hidden in the woods near the railroad tracks. Though he was persistent, he was unable to get any help.

The French, fearful lest they be German Gestapo agents, flirting disguise as Americans to locate underground members, would not believe ———'s [the pilot's] story nor offer any help of any kind. He returned to Slim with his report so they walked on some three or four more miles. With only canvas slippers, walking became torture to Slim whose feet were now badly bruised and blistered. The left one, tied on with a string, stayed on, but pain from Slim's wound was taking its toll in wearing down his resistance. They stopped again for some much needed rest.

Two flyers alone, set down by fate in a foreign land, in the midst of their enemies surrounding them on all sides. With the last refusal of help from their only source of help, they seemed doomed to the awaiting Gestapo's clutches. Tired and worn out, suffering from the shock of their last great battle for life itself, they sat and pondered what to do. Neither of them spoke or understood any French. Not knowing whether or not there was any help anywhere—Gestapo agents they had been told, went around as civilian French—what if they should by chance ask one of them—that surely would mean their end.

Hunger rapped loudly in their stomachs. They must do something soon in desperation if only to keep from starving. They sat in the open to one side of the highway. Coming down the highway in the distance they saw three bicycles approaching. Under the circumstances, there was little for them to do but sit and watch. The cyclists proved to be three young Frenchman who looked them over quizzically—two of them rode on past while the third one slowed down and began to whistle. Slim and ——— listened intently. The tune was "Tipperary." Slim sat up alert, staring after the boy. With waving hand and a broad smile the young Frenchman motioned to them to follow him. This they did for a while—down the highway without a word. Stopping, the French boy turned and waited for the flyers to catch up with them.

They used sign and motion to convey their need of help—the boy understood, promised to get a doctor, told them to wait there in the field. He rode on to his home and returned shortly with food and clothing—the food Slim and ——— were very happy to receive as they had not eaten since the day before. The boy, satisfied with his act, went home while Slim and ——— crossed into an oat field and slept until sundown. They soon came back again, this time with his father who took them three eighths of a mile across a field to their farmhouse where the wife received them. She dressed Slim's wound, poured whiskey over it, covered it with green leaves and bandaged it. The hand had been infected so bad by this time that he could hardly withstand anyone touching it. Although the medical treatment was somewhat crude, it eased the pain a little. Being thirsty they were given wine and Benedictine (a very rich French liquor, sweet and syrupy, clear as water).

They were taken to another nearby farmhouse where a French doctor soon arrived. He proceeded to amputate Slim's finger and dress it. This operation was quite painful but Slim permitted it to be done without flinching. They remained in this house all night. The doctor returned the next day to redress the wound. The bandage had so stuck to the wound that even after fifteen minutes of soaking it came off only with great difficulty, and much pain. Blood spurted from the finger's stump and was deftly stopped. They spent the following night and day here. As they watched from the house, their co-pilot ———— came walking toward them all alone. One of the Frenchmen leaped to the door and placed himself there defiantly so as to block any attempt of ———— to enter the house. Slim believed that, had they not convinced the Frenchman that———— was one of their party, he would have been killed. There are some among the French who would easily fight to the death for the safety of the one American flyer.

With ————'s arrival, they now had three in their escape party. It was as happy a reunion as one received back from the dead. [The] three of them stayed in this house all night and the next day, which was Tuesday. That night about 10 p.m., they started out on their journey again, with one Frenchman as a guide. He took them over fields and fences for miles. They came to an old railroad, which lay some three miles down a lane. On this railroad they walked more than ten miles at a fast pace—coming upon a fence crossing they stopped and were told to wait. The Frenchman left and returned fifteen minutes later bringing with him ————, the first engineer on Slim's crew. Their party then proceeded till they came to a highway where they were met by many young French boys with bicycles. These were used alternating with the Frenchman who followed close behind. Slim's feet had now become so blistered from walking in the canvas slippers that he could hardly travel at all.

"There is a path which no fool knoweth and which the vulture's eyes hath not seen, the lion's whelps have not trodden it nor the fierce lion pounced by it"— Job.

After walking for some distance they were met by a French police sergeant who joined the group. Turning off the highway onto a dirt road, they came into an orchard and stopped. Upon looking about amongst the men, they found the pilot missing. This created a great deal of excitement among the Frenchmen. The rest waited there while a young Frenchman was sent back along the road to look for him.

In such a perilous undertaking as this, it is necessary always to be on guard for roving German soldiers or agents of the Gestapo. For the general safety of the group they had previously arranged an alarm signal in the form of a word, which if given by the French guides meant the approach of the enemy and that the flyers should scramble over the road's embankment as quickly as possible.

The boy located ——— very quickly and upon his return, they learned that he [the pilot] had dived into the ditch upon thinking he heard the word given by the French in their normal conversation as they walked. After this narrow mix-up the understanding was straightened out and they proceeded towards a two story brick building near the orchard but not before ——— had received one of the most unique tongue lashings of his life by the young Frenchman who had gone back to find him.

At the brick building they found cider and wine. Being thirsty, they drank a lot. The police sergeant with them drank more than anyone, and repeatedly passed the bottle to Slim. It was Wednesday, near to two or three in the morning. Most of the Frenchmen left—only a farmer who lived in a house across the lane remained with them. He got a ladder, placed it against the building and took them up to the loft where they stayed. By this time Slim and the others had learned a few French words, those pertaining to food, mostly. Each day as food was brought to them the Frenchman took away the ladder to the loft so they were forced to remain in it all during the day. They talked some but mostly slept.

Early Friday morning the French police sergeant came after them. They walked then approximately one quarter of a mile from the lane to the highway. As they trod along someone yelled the signal.

Over the embankment went the crew, hurriedly seeking cover. This scare proved only to be a passing wagon. Returning to the road they walked on to an awaiting French car. They got in with the sergeant and the driver.

For most of the day they rode in what seemed to Slim as circles. Soon after they began riding, flat tire trouble began. One after another of the tires would blow out due to the overloaded car. Each time they stopped to fix the tire, the sergeant would not allow any of the Americans out to help. The last time they stopped, another French car pulled to a stop in front of them. Two men jumped out of the car. As they neared them, Slim recognized one of them as ————, the ball turret gunner. He was overjoyed to see them and had much to tell but they had little time then for conversation. Slim and the co-pilot were put in the front car to relieve the pressure on the worn tires of their first car. Slim knew not where the rest of the crew were taken but he and the co-pilot were taken to the home of a butcher in a town called ————, where they were given plenty of food to eat. The butcher was supposedly the head of the French [underground] in that district. There was a boy in the house who could speak a little English. In their stay at this house, the Germans gave them many uneasy moments. However, on such occasions, they received helpful reassurances as the boy would say to them, "It's all right. We have pistols: we take care of them." There were other roomers in this house, among whom were two German soldiers living in the front rooms upstairs—while the flyers stayed in the back rooms on the same floor. A doctor came and re-dressed Slim's hand. It was in a bad condition. Later more clothing was brought, with a special made pair of shoes for Slim. These shoes gave reason for humor among the neighboring folk of strangers, being guests of the house. There was somewhat a stir caused by this in the household for fear the Gestapo might hear of it.

Two days later at another house where the whole crew was again assembled, the French took back the shoes. The crew learned after that the particular man who talked was "taken care of." At this house they received excellent food and wine. Two beautiful French girls, daughters of the household, lived here. They spent most of their time laughing at the Americans' sad attempt to learn French. Their stay was short, for early the next morning another Frenchman came after them. The building was of a horseshoe shape. In the center drive was the truck they were to leave in. As they walked out they were told to lie down amongst the baggage on the truck bed facing the front. This they did while the driver very cleverly spaced the baggage among them and covered them with a canvas top making the whole thing appear as a load of trunks. The surprising part of it was that all of the plan of concealment was carried out directly below all the windows of the house from which anyone could have observed very easily the business at hand.

They rode what seemed to be about three quarters of an hour. Having given their watches to the French previously, they did not know the exact time. The truck turned off the road. They felt as though they were riding down a hill, although they weren't sure since no one dared show his head in looking out. Finally the truck rolled to a stop. They could hear the cab door slam. Some time elapsed possibly three or four minutes—then the canvas was thrown back. The driver stood motioning them to get out. They were at a store or some kind of a warehouse on the side of a steep hill along which ran a stream. Another Frenchman appeared, the drivers' brother, and they were taken inside the house. It was a flour mill owned by the two brothers ———. Here they lived all alone with a housekeeper and a mill hand. The mill was adjoined to the two and a half story house and was run by the water power of the stream. Their stay here was a brief interlude of enjoyment for most of the crew, who were permitted to fish and boat on the stream. Slim was always kept in the house because of his unusual stature. The French were fearful that someone passing might take notice of this to the extent of passing the information along with some remark in a saloon. Though not out of suspicion on the part of the person, such a casual remark might to the Gestapo mean a great deal. On this they took no chance. Slim stayed inside.

In their stay here, they learned many things concerning conditions in Europe. All food in Belgium, France, and Holland was under the most strict rations. It was practically impossible to get even the barest of necessities by their system, hence the great trade was carried on through the "Black Market" without the limit of ration cards, etc. With George, the elder of the two brothers, having a mill where many customers came daily, it was easy to carry on such a trade. The crew lacked nothing that could be had. There was always tobacco, butter, and good food at their disposal during their stay. One morning the French commissioned with other Frenchmen came and talked for quite some time to Johnnie and George. A doctor arrived and Slim's hand was attended to. With the commissioner came more clothing and a new pair of dress shoes for Slim. During all this time, Pilot ——— had remained at the butcher's place, the home of the two girls and came out on a bicycle to see the rest of the crew only occasionally. They had not as yet heard any news of the fate of the other crew members.

From the French they learned only that the plane had burned, that possibly one of the crew was dead and the other one in a French hospital.

A photographer was brought in and each crew member received a card with their photo and fictitious names which they were told was their passport. Everyone in Europe, it seems, must have "papers," passport or work cards for identification. Their laundry at this house was all done by the housekeeper.

On Friday June the eleventh at about 4 p.m. the crew was taken by truck towards town. This time they were not concealed by canvas, but rode openly dressed in their new civilian clothes. At last they rode with the feeling of greater security. At times with the hope of freedom so strong within them that they could put out of their minds for a few seconds the nerve-wracking strain of the desperate journey, they watched the peaceful French countryside roll past with its farms and churches. These moments of imaginary freedom were quickly vanished at the sight of a passing German soldier. These passing glimpses of the enemy soon brought their minds back to the realm of stark reality. They neared the town and rolled on into the crowded streets without slacking their speed. On they went at what seemed to be a reckless speed, through the swarm of pedestrians and cyclists barely missing them as they crossed in front of the truck. Cows, sheep, goats, and chickens were among those unmindful of the speeding truck. A block from the railroad station, the truck stopped and they got out. Following the driver they crossed the street, entered a saloon and walked through it amongst the tables of German drinking parties.

Upstairs they entered a room where another German stood to meet them. There were a few instructions given to the saloon owner by the driver in French, which Slim and the others understood. The driver soon departed leaving them with the saloon owner. Slim noticed at once the unusual behavior of this fellow. In a nervous agitating manner he bustled about, at the same time wiping the great beads of sweat that dripped from his forehead. Since it was rather cool, Slim could hardly understand his being so warm. The Germans who crowded the saloon downstairs had merely glanced at the flyers as they passed through. Slim paid no more attention to the slight twitch of suspicion he had just experienced. They remained in the room for about one hour while the Frenchmen went out. Returning shortly he brought train tickets for each man. He then took three of them down to the train, went back and brought out the other two men.

Before the driver left them, he gave them three packages containing food. These they took with them to the train. The Frenchmen were to go with them on their trip to Paris. Slim and the others found seats in the crowded car while the Frenchmen stood up at one end of the car. The train was very old and very slow. They rode along fully one hour before they reached the next station for more passengers. From the train window Slim noticed the sign on the station "St. Nickelus." There was the usual wait for passengers getting off and on. As they shifted about to accommodate the new passengers, one young fellow in a checked suit planted himself directly in front of "Slim." Slim, with head bowed, stared at the floor as though half asleep in hopes of avoiding any forced conversation. As he stared, something caught his eye which gave him an inward start, though he showed no outward sign of it. The shoes this fellow was wearing were highly familiar to him.

Yes, he was sure of it! They were United States Army regulation shoes. As Slim had been noticing the familiar shoes, the train had moved on and was now coming to a stop some two hundred yards from the station. Possibly switching, he thought. But no someone was yelling "heads up," "heads up." Slim's head came up from his supposed drowsing. And from out of nowhere pistols appeared dangerously pointed at his face. Menacing lugars, here was a story told without asking. The whole crew sat dazed, this just couldn't be—but here it was staring them in the face.

Captured by the Gestapo. Their fine friend and aid, the saloon owner, they saw standing foremost among the Gestapo agents—jabbering away. Germans pointing first to one member of the crew, then another. The young man who had been standing in front of Slim turned with upraised hands. He too was caught. One grand haul for the Gestapo. The door of the train next to Slim flew open with a bang. As he looked out, there in rank and file stood what seemed to Slim, the entire German Army. It all happened so fast. Slim and the crew were greatly confused, and said nothing. The Gestapo began handcuffing the crew, as they screamed to Slim to put out his hands, he drew from his coat his wounded hand in a black bandage. The German Gestapo agents followed it closely with their lugars, perhaps expecting to see a gun. Slim was handcuffed and the entire crew, including the young man in the checked suit, were turned over to the awaiting German guards. It was a sad procession of disheartened American flyers who were marched back to the station. All because of one dirty traitor amongst a perfect syndicate of loyal brave French people. No better chance would they ever again have, under the watchful vigilance of the German guards. Thus their most dreaded fear had fallen upon them, out of a clear sky without warning to snatch from them their only hope of escape and return to England.

All of their carefully planned escape and struggle snapped by one single traitor. This they saw with unmerciful irony and bitterness as they marched back, prisoners of the Germans.

> "What though the field be lost?
> All is not lost. The conquerable will
> and study of revenge, immortal hate
> and courage never to submit or yield
> and what else is not to be overcome."
> —MILTON

The courage that does not flinch when the field is lost the instance of a soul . . .with undimmed brightness beneath the cares of the world and the dust of conflict and the savage triumph of the enemy—the inheritance of free Americans their only remaining ray of hope and light which was to prove their cause to the Germans who looked into hideous eyes for the chance of ending their lives or the breaking down of strong young men of America under their barbarous treatment and imprisonment.

They were taken back to the rear of the station where the bus stood. Sitting in all the seats next to the windows were more German guards. They were forced into the bus and sat in the seats next to the aisle. The bus soon rolled out onto the highway. No words were exchanged between the prisoners and the guards. The standing guard only stared—Slim returned the stare. Out along the highway they traveled at a terrific speed. A small herd of cattle driven by a peasant loomed up on the road ahead. The driver made no effort to avoid the poor animals. The bus plowed unmercifully through them, leaving their carcasses spread all over the road. This to the Germans was a great joke, and they laughed uproariously. Shortly afterward a car came zooming past the bus with the occupants waving madly. It pulled ahead and the bus and car stopped. Another prisoner, accompanied by the same traitor who sealed the doom of Slim and the crew. They stopped at this spot for nearly an hour with nothing happening. A few French civilians came up walking slowly, stopped, and looked quizzically at the men in the bus. The Germans waved their guns at them and sent them on their way.

The bus rolled on and in a short while stopped at the police station at the town of Pontivic. Here Slim and the crew were taken into a large room and seated in straight back chairs lined up facing the wall. One by one the flyers were taken out by a guard into an office and questioned by an English-speaking officer. The Officer wanted to know among other things—where they had received the civilian clothing. From whom did they obtain help—how long ago were they shot down, etc. When Slim was taken in, out of curiosity, the German officer demanded to see the wounded hand. He proceeded savagely to tear off the bandage, which came off only after very much effort not to mention the pain. Satisfied with this, he made an even worse attempt at re-bandaging it. Slim asked whether he would allow him to bandage it himself, but the German only laughed sarcastically, enjoying this hurt he was inflicting on the American. After the questioning they sat silent in the big room. ———, with legs crossed, began tapping the wall unconsciously. With a mad flurry one German stepped forward and savagely struck him across the legs a terrific blow with a long rod. ——— said nothing but ——— turned in indignation to speak—he also received the same treatment. Slim, out of the corner of his eye, noticed another prisoner sitting in the end chair with bowed head. After a closer observance he saw it was the police commissioner who had helped them. Here in the chairs, the prisoners sat and tried to sleep from 4 p.m. until 9. a.m., with the guards continually poking them to keep them awake. They received no food during this time. Presently the guards took them outside to the bus. As Slim got on, he noticed there were already other prisoners aboard. The two French brothers, Johnnie and George, who helped them, two women and an old man. The two brothers sat weeping.

They drove some two or three hours to the prison at Rennen. Here the crew was taken upstairs to a small cell. Altogether there had been fifteen people from the underground picked up in connection with the flyers [who] attempted escape. Hungry, they asked for food, which the Germans promised to bring. About an hour later towards noon they returned with hard tack biscuits, a round gob of cheese, the size of a nickel pie, "moldy" and three dirty broken eggs that they refused to eat. They were soon to regret this fate, for starvation was something new in this place, which they had not yet experienced.

The German guards then came and wanted any three of the crew who wished to stay together to come with them. ———, ———, and ——— went together while Slim ——— and the new member, Lieutenant Colonel ——— remained. Up to this time, the crew had said little or nothing among themselves. Since their last encounter with a traitor, they were not so quick to take up with a stranger, fearing further treachery. The first three were sent to one cell while Slim, ———, and the new member Lieutenant Colonel ——— remained. Later they were put in another cell. Slim and the others by this time were both very hungry and worn out. In this prison they were kept thirteen anxious days. The food was terrible. In the morning at ten o'clock they were given cabbage and water soup. They could not eat the cabbage but drank the juice for it was hot. Bread was made by the French, a dark, moldy tasteless stuff, rationed one and a half loaf a day for three men. At 4 o'clock the Germans gave them soup made of barley and water. The latrine was a can set into a hole in the wall. The walls were made of white limestone some two or three feet in thickness. The emptying of the latrines was done by French slaves who would slide open a door opposite the can and take it out daily. From this opening, "Slim" could see the slaves carrying stacks of cans as tall as themselves. On the prison cell door was a slot with a small sliding panel through which the guards frequently peeped in to see what the prisoners were doing. There was but one window in the cell about one foot square. One small, hinged bunk hung from the wall by chains. This was the sleeping accommodations for three men. Two of them slept on the floor. They received a bit of fresh air once a day when they were taken outdoors for fifteen minutes. Rat holes dotted the walls. Each night when they would go to sleep the rats would run freely all over the cell. On some days Slim was taken upstairs where he received some medical treatment for his hand. It was not long before ——— had established his identity with Slim and the others so they talked with one another quite freely. ——— slept most of the time. Slim and ——— slept very little. The arrival at the prison had been on June 12th, 1943 and it was June 24th before they were taken by bus to the station and sent on their way to the Paris civilian prison. The trip was very long, taking them more than ten hours to get there. There was no chance of escape while on this trip as the guards watched them continually.

PARIS PRISON

Upon arrival at the French prison they were walked between double walls eighteen feet high. The prison itself was in three divisions. They were taken through underground tunnels and passages so confusing that they were all mixed up by the time they arrived at the third division. The building was five stories high, and Slim was quartered on the fifth floor, with a window facing east. The first night they were given a large bowl of soup. Guards came into each cell and had the prisoners remove their clothing and a thorough search was made. Even the seams in their clothing were cut open. They confiscated their belts, shoe strings, and ties to prevent them from committing suicide by hanging. The walls in the prison between the cells were some three feet thick and the outside [wall] was about four feet thick. Not a sound could be heard between the cells. The next day they took ———— out of his cell and the Germans tore up the floor looking for anything he might have hidden. Under the loose boards they found a long knife. It was a French army knife almost a foot long. At one end of the prison Slim could see women prisoners out for their daily promenade. One day the prisoners were lined up and the Germans told them that if they abided by the rules they might be placed three in a cell. Slim asked what the rules consisted of. They were asked not to shout out the windows, mark on the walls, look out the windows, not to pass conversation down the ventilator shaft, [to] sweep the floor and whenever an officer entered their cell they were to stand at attention. They agreed to these rules with their fingers crossed. Slim was put in one cell with ————, ————, while ————, ————, and ———— were put in another. The cell had one, one-man bunk loaded with fleas and bedbugs. Two had to sleep on the floor. There was one frosted glass window which was locked. The latrine was in the cell, a bowl which had to be used standing up was also a part of the cell's makeup. There was also a water spout above the bowl. Water could be obtained by pressing a button on the wall. There were two shelves on which they kept their eating utensils (a tin can and wooden spoon). A stool and a table hinged to the wall made up the completion of the cell's furniture. Food was brought about seven o'clock—coffee (burnt), and barley juice, half a can.

At 9:30 a.m. the trash can came around. At 11:30 they received their ration of bread (half a loaf for three men), strong very old margarine, and a piece of meat 4" by 2" by ¾" thick. It was horsemeat and mostly gristle. Soup was given them twice a week along with a little bit of cottage cheese. Sometimes they received a little watery jam at 4:00 P.M. They had acorn coffee (with no supper). They had no tobacco and all in their party but one were heavy smokers. After a short while the slightest noise was like a long speech to them. They got to know exactly what was going on by the noises the Germans made outside their cell door.

———— paced the floor from morning till night. There were worn out places in the exact spots where his footsteps marked the floor. ———— sat and talked but sometimes he would pace the floor for an hour or so just to keep ———— off ————. It got on their nerves so much it became unbearable at times. ————, ————, and ———— talked mostly of planes and people they knew in training. From June 29th until October 1st they received civilian rations, which were most meager. On military rations they received three cigarettes a day. Slim lost very much weight, as did the others under these conditions. They could communicate with the other prisoners by mean[s] of the ventilating shaft.

An English man occupied a cell below theirs who was serving a turn of six months. "George Ross 33 Stantry Road, West Croyden, England." ———— discouraged the use of code as Slim was a Radio Operator. There was always someone pounding the walls. Most news the prisoners received was from this Englishman. Since they called him George, he called them America. George learned French and somehow got a great deal of news through the French. They called him almost anytime during the day. Another American was put into Slim's cell, a First Lieutenant. Dressed in "pinks," he was a pilot. They also brought in an English Second Lieutenant, and placed him in the other cell with the rest of the crew. This Englishman went to school in America, trained in Canada, flew with the R.A.F. and spoke French. The Lieutenant in Slim's cell came from Mississippi. His name was Wheat Bull. ———— came from San Angelo, Texas. These new arrivals made it four in each cell. ———— slept in the bunk until the fleas got so bad he tried the floor. They had two badly torn blankets each. There was no heating system at all in the prison, at times it was so cold they all huddled on the edge on the bunk wrapped in blankets.

Wheat was taken out one day and never brought back. The next day the Germans put a Belgian civilian in the cell with them who spoke French,

English and Flemish. He was of average height, well-built, very muscular. Not a day went by that he didn't exercise and always before the rest of them awoke. Standing nude, he would always massage himself until his skin would turn red. The only one of them who would sit completely down on the latrine, take a cold can of water and pour it over his privates, and under his arms. Slim and the others would watch him with indignation. His favorite expression which also got on their nerves was "Dem it all" which he would say over and over. He was a great believer and ready for arguments on the Bible. Born in England and for some reason refused by the English Army, he came to Belgium where he lived for fifteen years. Upon the coming of the second World War, he passed for a Belgian but for some reason had to hide from the authorities. When the Germans marched through Belgium he began his escapade of hiding, finally falling into the hands of the Gestapo.

When the bread was divided by the Germans, it was cut into equal shares, except whenever the knife fell carelessly on the piece. When men are forced to live so close under such trying conditions, with very little food and not knowing what day their number would be up, there are bound to be minor frictions among such close association. Though small at first, they will grow in importance. An empty stomach is a hard thing to cope with and the strain of keeping one's self control is harder still to bear.

There was very little food. Each crumb of bread was swept off the boards and eaten. ———, being senior officer, took over in full from the beginning, which was all right with Slim, being under his command and recognizing his capacity and responsibility as an officer. Each day he would stand by the door and receive the food rations. He would carefully examine each bit in size and give the other men the smaller pieces, keeping the largest for himself. This went on day after day without Slim or the others saying anything about it. A pail of jam was brought to them one day and each man was to get what they had prearranged to take with all sincerity as their share. On that particular day Slim had received his smallest of bread rations from ———. ——— took what Slim thought [was] more than his share of the jam. Slim mentioned the fact but ——— pretended to overlook the matter. When ——— heard this he gave a chuckle and Slim soon realized he was alone. So Slim talked to no one at all for a while. Later, ——— demanded an explanation for Slim's behavior. The others argued amongst themselves. Slim argued that he had every right to say something about it and would not take back what he said. He would have said more had the incident provoked it. They ironed out their difficulties by letting all take part in the rationing program. Living so close, the officer ———— could easily see that his was an overbearing appearance towards the others. His attitude turned seemingly to that, he deserved more than the others. An individual right, in his own mind. Relations among them were becoming more and more strained. For almost a month, ———— had not spoken to Slim. Later, however, they made up and sided together against Watter the Belgian on any subject of discussion.

———— would stand on Watter's shoulders and yell to the rest of the crew to keep contact as to how they were getting along. Most of what they learned was what ———— had heard from the other English prisoners of what the Germans did to them. They were beaten up, handcuffed, kicked in the groin, thoroughly flogged in order to gain information. There was a Hungarian prisoner who jumped out of the fifth story window and died as the result. He also had been beaten up so badly that he feared he might weaken and give the names of his associates, so he committed suicide.

Any time an air raid alarm sounded, the Germans locked up all the French prisoners and made themselves scarce to the air raid shelters below. If the all-clear did not sound at night, they did not pull the prisoners.

In a cell next to theirs were fourteen French prisoners, civilians condemned to die for sabotage to a trainload of German troops. Because of their status, they received parcels of food from their friends and relatives. Some of the contents of these parcels were passed to Slim and his friends through a fairly humane guard.

On October ninth, Slim and the crew left the Paris prison for a place at that time unknown to them. Later they learned from a guard that they were going to Dulag Luft in Frankfurt, Germany. At Dulag Luft they went through their interrogation to no avail, as far as the Germans were concerned.

A few days later they left Frankfurt for Krems, Austria. This time they traveled in true "Kriegie" fashion, in a box car 40 and 8. On October 19th, Slim arrived at Stalag XVII B, one of the many German prison camps for American flyers. In his own words, Slim says, "This place is heaven compared to the prison in Paris."

If this is what he calls Heaven, I am glad I never saw the prison in Paris.

Joe Hafer

Carano wrote the following sketch to accompany his portrait of Joe Hafer, which he drew on September 23, 1944. Hafer autographed the portrait with a sweeping, "Joseph E. Hafer."

First Radio Operator—"Brady's Crash Wagon." Shot down over Munster, October 10, 1943 (16th mission). Five years Army life, Two years a Boxer, 5' 4" ?, 142 lbs.

Joe set a good example of undaunted American spirit and stubborn unwillingness to concede one inch to our Nazi captors. Had two weeks of solitary for the best attempt at escape from XVII B, January 18 in the middle of the winter. Before the Germans caught him, Joe had forty miles between him and the prison. His favorite habit is chewing cigarettes, poker and all. Joe received the Air Medal with two oak leaf clusters before he was shot down, has a great sense of humor, but it isn't wise to rub Joe the wrong way.

"JOSEPH E. HAFER"
(1801 TALIFANO ST.
TAMPA, FLORIDA)

SEPTEMBER 27TH, 1944

Writing by Comrades

Carano's journal paid homage to men in Stalag XVII B, not only by recording their stories and their faces, but by providing a forum for the men to write their own essays and poetry. The subject didn't matter to Carano— it could be either the mundane or the sentimentally sublime—what mattered was the sense of comaraderie that emerged from the theater of his journal. In these pages, he created both a private retreat for himself and a public space for his friends.

Some of the most demoralizing moments in Stalag XVII came not from German propaganda but from an occasional letter from home denigrating the men for having been captured—attitudes the Germans must have been glad to read when they censored the mail. Infuriated by comments that came to their comrades from girlfriends, wives, or even their parents, the "Kriegies" wrote poems, letters, and essays of outrage. Having endured both the daring, bloody battles in the sky over Europe and the traumas of capture and imprisonment, they understood that both required inner strength and courage. The two following essays were written by two of Carano's comrades about the attitudes of some of their fellow Americans on the home front. The first ironically signs himself as "Quitter," and the second, the author of "A Kriegie's Reply," chose to remain anonymous.

WHAT A PRICE TO PAY

What a price to pay for no Glory. For here in a prison camp there is no one hero. They are all heroes. And any man that fights to defend democracy, and America which stands for democracy, is no common hero. For such is the war of today, this modern war in which the individual is expendable. A great homage should be paid to those who live through the hours of war. The Greatest Homage should be paid to those who have succumbed to the wickedness of war.

Why are there wars?

Why are there prisons for people to fight for freedom?

Why do the Germans treat us so?

If only the U.S. public cared a damn of what happens to us—but no! Some are too busy thinking of themselves to give a P. O. W. a thought.

And to prove it, some wives and girlfriends have written to P. O. W.s calling us quitters.

Someday they may know!

Upon the following pages is the answer to all those ignorant asses (for I can't call them people) who wrote letters to P. O. W.s here calling them quitters and sending them such things as white and yellow feathers, which symbolize cowardice. The people who wrote such letters aren't the ones my buddies and I fought for. They were the type who tear down what you strive to erect. Yet they are the ones who are the boastful loudmouths who are winning the war for us, working in some toy factory back home, never knowing death, never seeing men killed or suffering the horror of war. All they know is gaiety and laughter while men die.

The majority of letters received here from home were written by "Girlfriends" and a few by some fellows' parents. One "father" (if he can be called that) wrote his son never to come home again, as he was not welcome, for he was a quitter. Girlfriends even wrote, "You're a yellow-bellied quitter otherwise you wouldn't be a prisoner; you gave up. So I am marrying a man with courage, a Lieutenant in the O.M.C." This Lieutenant must have been a brave soldier who never saw action, yet knows all about war.

These people disgust me so I'll stop here. My only upset is that they aren't the ones who are dead instead of some of the quitters who gave their lives in order that trash like that might live in a free land of Democracy.

(QUITTER, P.O.W. 100576)

A KRIEGIE'S REPLY

You say that we are quitters, we haven't got the guts it takes to stand up and die.

But I'll just try to tell you a part of the hell they have to go through. "The boys who fly." The Jerries make it hot up there—but of course you know. You've seen the flak bursting—in the local movie show. We've seen the Focke-Wolfes cannon flash as he dashed in for the kill, and we couldn't line our sights up as the devil wouldn't stand still. We've lined them up though; yes, and blew them all to hell! We took our share of Jerries, also tasted all their hell. We've seen Fortune blown to bits and pieces go bursting downward. We've fought in the Stratosphere, and also in our dreams. Midst all the flak and fighters we've heard the pilot say, "Controls are gone! Two engines out, get ready to bail out." The kid in the tail had long since been dead, a 20 M.M. got him [in] the head. You glance at your buddy in the waist, yes another dead!

The engines whine with a hell of a roar, your ship is plunging for the ground, the kid in the ball turret that little "luminum ball" struggles to release himself through all this fearful fall.

At last you got your chute on and struggle for the door, but you're pinned in the plane and hear the whine and roar. Then your ship blows to pieces and you "black out." You come to with your chute on and you're floating to the ground. From twenty thousand feet up the wind twists round and round, and it takes you near half an hour before you hit the ground.

There you find a dozen Jerries each with an evil gloat. They know you've bombed their homes and they would like to cut your throat. You haven't got a weapon and you can't even stand up to run, but if it was you, "my hero," I bet you would have some fun. I could go on and tell you more of this sad tale, cause when the Jerries want to they make even brave men quail.

Now where did I get these stories? That's what I want to tell.

They're gathered from my buddies round me, in a German prison cell.

Some with arms or legs shot off, some who cannot see.

But every man here has done his part, to preserve Democracy.

Their fighting days are over, and in my mind there's no doubt
If everyone would do as much, we'd soon have the Jerry out.

P. O. W.
KREMS, AUSTRIA

THE FLEA EPIC

Challenges to the men in Stalag XVII B came in many forms: through the shocking denunciations of them in hateful letters from home or through a vicious attack of fleas, which could be enough to nearly drive a man mad. In "The Flea Epic," Carano's comrade Jim Watkins recorded a harrowing episode with what many might see as a minor nuisance: fleas. For Watkins, the insects' relentless attacks each night drove him to a maddening state of battling bites and sleeplessness. In the flea-ridden straw "palliases" in the barracks, fleas were practically an epidemic that might strain a prisoner's sanity with lack of rest and incessant itching. When the prisoners most needed their mental acuity and rest, the fleas became yet another enemy, an insidious form of torture invented by nature.

Although there are some petty tyrannies of the Jerries to put up with, one can gain something over the experience which nerve-provoking hardships provide. Such was the case in my encounter with German fleas and lice, which were so active in the beds and walls when we first came to this camp. It went on for some three months [before] the Jerries got around to ridding our abode of these devils and a more miserable experience I never wish to experience again. They played great havoc with me in particular but very few were exempt from their mighty menace. Night after night I was attacked incessantly with no let-up, or any sign of relief. I was completely covered with bites of all sizes and description.

The straw palliases on which we slept and the rotten wood of the bunks and barracks afforded a good living quarters for the fleas, lice, bugs and all other known types of German vermin. After three months I still bear scars from their bites . . . Like everything else, we made attempts to joke and laugh it off in the truest American style, but these bugs were more than persistent. They, like their two-legged brothers, are not so easily laughed off, or burned, as we tried them all, and many other, means, including white-washing the walls and bunks, soaping the boards, etc.

Scratching the bites was what made matters worse. I am convinced that I'm not so "shilly-shally" that my willpower cannot resist any temptation within reason, but not scratching a flea bite was a lot more than I could take. Due to the run-down condition of my body, due to malnutrition, I was unable to fight infection and made many sick calls to our infirmary, where I saw some serious cases of infected flea bites among our fellow prisoners. Due to the fact that we get baths only once a month, once the fleas are on you it may be a month before you can wash them off and I was too damned cold to risk a wash under a faucet. By the time I tried my act of sleeping on a table they had gained full control of my blankets and clothing.

The strangest part of the whole affair was that my bed partner did not get one bite while I could not find a single place on my body that was not gleaned of red corpuscles. He slept on peacefully each night, while I tossed, scratched and cursed myself into complete exhaustion. The only time I slept was when I had worn myself out slapping, trying to get rid of the critters, and then it wouldn't have mattered to me if the barracks had burned down.

Relief finally came when the Jerries moved us to another barracks and deloused ours, but I'm sure, despite the gas, that some of the fleas escaped to the foothills.

Jim Watkins
P.O.W., Krems, Austria
1943–1944

"KURT" KURTENBACH

Carano preserved speeches and sermons in his journal, including this one by Stalag XVII B's "Man of Confidence," Kenneth J. "Kurt" Kurtenbach. Elected by his fellow prisoners of war, the "Man of Confidence" in each stalag was entrusted to take their grievances to the Germans in the camp and to the Red Cross when they made inspections. Not necessarily the senior-ranking POW, the "MOC" also occasionally helped the men make plans to escape. Kurtenbach's strong leadership, intelligence, and charisma can be seen in the following speech and poetry recitation recorded in Carano's diary.

The following is a speech made by Kurtenbach, Stalag camp leader, one who is looked upon with great respect by every man in Stalag XVII B.

Comrades and true Americans—the fortunes of war have made us much-exiled from home and loved ones, but the triumphant American spirit that we have shown here at this Stalag is one that nothing can daunt. I believe I have an excerpt from one of Stephen Benet's poems that expresses a thought common to us all—expresses more significantly that torn and tattered as we may be, our American spirit carries on. Some may call it "G.I." Some may call it that "Air Corps" but still we know what it is. Let these last stanzas of "The Winged Man" carry your thoughts for these remaining days.

On the highest steps of space, he will have his dwelling place,
In these far terrible regions, where the cold comes down like death,
Gleams the red glint of his pinions smokes the vapor of his breath.
Floating downward very clear still the echoes reach the ear,

Of a little tune he whistles of a little song he sings.
Mounting, mounting, still triumphant on his torn and broken wings.

Yes, comrades, our wings are torn and broken, but still as in this poem comes that little whistled tune, and that little song. Still, we carry on with the traditions and the ideals as laid down by the makers of our country on that great Fourth of July 1776. You at home in America had your sporting events and your familiar traditional songs. But America, we, too, had our 4th of July with the full herd of every man in camp, and in every sporting event, in every note of music, we were with you.

Today we stopped for a breather to remember the old traditions, and to remember the ideals that the 4th of July means to us all. We stopped and saw that each man next to us, was an American with the same hopes and ambitions as our own. We saw, too, that he remembered the principles for which we stand. We pause here for a moment to remind you, America, and to remind ourselves, that although we are enclosed by a barbed wire fence and ringed by our enemies, and although we have broken wings, our spirits still and will fly high.

Feel confident, America, that we are ever more convinced now, of the worth and merit of your ideals. We know now, and will never forget, the blessings of a country formed of the people, by the people, for the people. With the coming peace, we will return to your shores, dogged by determination to see the rights of citizenship observed and protected. We still strive to the best of our ability to see that another such crisis does not occur. And we will to a man, return with a deeper more lasting appreciation of your principles and ideals, your rights and standards. And this above all, we will return with a deep respect and sincere appreciation of our fundamental privileges—Independence. Believe us—we came, we saw, were convinced.

> Yes, America
> Broken wings, floating downward, very clear still
> the echoes reach the ear.
> Of a little tune he whistles, and a little song he sings.
> Mounting, mounting, still triumphant on his
> torn and broken wings.

—KENNETH KURTENBACH
JULY 4, 1944

FATHER KANE

Father Stephen Kane, an Army captain, was the only chaplain in Stalag XVII, where he led services for Catholic and Protestant inmates and held daily communion. His sermons and stories helped build morale among the soldiers, sometimes bearing a mystical message about the power of faith. It was not unusual for soldiers to report a sense of "otherworldliness," or what they called spiritual guidance, during battle or injury. Carano, who obviously admired Kane a great deal, had had his own strange vision of his family when he nearly drowned beneath his plane as it sank off the coast of Holland, a mental image that gave him the sudden power to wrench himself free from the wreckage holding him beneath the water.

In "Strange But True," Carano writes about how Kane used his Catholic mysticism to bolster the morale of the troops. (Unknown to the Germans, and possibly unknown to Carano as well, a Jewish prisoner of war, Roke Lieberman, led regular, clandestine services for the Jewish soldiers held in the camp.)

Strange But True

The strangest story I have ever heard or read was written by Father Kane, who was at one time a prisoner in Poland. The reliability of the story is beyond question—of Father Kane's own personal experience and his word of honor [is] unreproachable.

Three million brave soldiers crushed in defeat—Poland's famous mounted troops had made the last charge, but new weapons of war be thanked and a slumbering paradise reproved in forgetting eternal vigilance at the price of peace. All the horrors of tyranny came swiftly to a vanquished nation. A blitzkrieg, they called it, and quickly and efficiently to the minutest detail was every vestige of Polish culture doomed to destruction. The wayside shrines, sacred those hundreds of years to a religious Poland, were not last to share the fate of Prussian terror. In the district of Kemper, where we happened to be imprisoned at the time of writing, and close by the village of Mechau, the grand work of destroying superstition had begun.

English prisoners of war were directed to pull down statues, to clear away offensive crucifixion scenes. Not alone came the common answer—no good can come of this. English Protestant "Tommies" refused, even with threats of death, to touch except in reverence, those shrines sacred to the Catholic belief. The square headed "good" was in charge of the group of English lads who persistently refused to carry out the orders of the Third Reich. Klose decided on a personal exhibition of Boche efficiency, and with his companions, German guards, quickly knocked down the roadside crucifix. The expert methods of Jerry's superior brain needed further display. A four-minute conference and the best stroke, and least labor, and the task would be complete for the edification of prisoners who must of course accept the recognition of a superior race. It was an excellent job, with one brilliant stroke. Klose severed the right arm of the bronze corpse. A master stroke that left little for soldier Luffler to do in completely splitting lengthwise, the remains of what once reminded passing generations of the infamy of Golgotha.

A great day's work complete and haughty guards assembled the group of "commandos" for the march back to quarters. It was a sad and sullen group, strangely led by two German heroes. Two kilometers against the cold wind and little attention was paid to a familiar railroad sign. There was a sudden swish and the momentary commotion gave emphasis to a strange scene of mangled blue clad corpses. The "Tommies" went back to verify the picture of a previous hour. Yes, it was too true. Kloses' head and arm lay in the identical position of that bronze head and arm, while Luffler lay neatly and lengthwise split beside the Polish crossing. It was true, Tommy, no good can come of this, but the ways of providence are strange as sometimes the mills grind slow.

Only the Actions of the Just Smell Sweet and Blossom in Their Dust

Taken from the writings of Father Kane—who in words can better than any man describe the thoughts of P.O.W.s who lack in education and understanding, a way that is most useful in expressing what is in their minds and hearts.

No place else in all creation gives the opportunities of character study as does the prison camp. Clear as the windowpane is the make-up, the worth and general character of the average prisoner. Gold is purified by fire, the man's real character is stripped of all artificialities and only the genuinely worthwhile can maintain the even tenor of ways that credit mankind. The general selfishness of our creative make-up becomes so patently evident that even the most self-centered have good reason . . . to double-check on tendencies that wreak havoc in community life. The evil is so heinous that the blindest are forced to the recognition of the smallest symptoms of selfishness and the opposite virtues are perforce given an excellent chance to develop into life-long habits. We must develop in ourselves those qualities most admired in others.

Carano recorded Father Kane's reflections on how the prisoner of war survives emotionally and psychologically, apparently from one of Kane's sermons.

Is It A Sudden Maturing?

It must be the dozen life experiences packed into weeks that so quickly sum up and evaluate individual worth. There may be no art to find [the] mind's construction in the face, but our empty stomachs will quickly transmit the worth of any "guy." Not every day, but every minute of each hour is the ever-present opportunity with each prisoner to destroy the ego in self by the generous dealing with fellow prisoners. One cannot blame too severely the white-livered character of the born coward, but none will justify the rapacious self-centered in character that instantly evidences itself in every thought and action of the most despised creature in camp, that selfish guy.

Greatness of heart, magnanimity of soul must needs find a home in the person of every "gefangenen" [captive]. Opposing tendencies stand not as billboard posters that even the most indifferent are bound to read and profit thereby. A man must of necessity be many times a better man, because of these gray days that will soon even give proper background to the years in Rose and Gold that all so patiently anticipate.

This life of a "Kriegie" had taught me that one hour's liberty is worth an eternity of bondage and the ideas of freedom—democracy—once vague abstract ideas are tangible concrete realities in the America we left. Our liberties are great but manufactured of men with the intellect, the heart, and the will of "Johnny Doughboy" and the might of Uncle Sam.

S. KANE

POETRY

Writing verse gave the POWs a private forum to express their pain at the deaths of their buddies in combat, frustration over the poor mattresses where they slept, and, of course, their memories of home.

Sentimental poetry was a typical expression of loneliness for the soldiers in captivity. The form freed the writers to express a range of emotions they otherwise would perhaps not so readily have exposed, from intimate messages to their loved ones to rage against their captors. Carano's pages became a place where the men could see their work "published" in Carano's meticulous handwriting, and sometimes illustrated. One of the poets whose work Carano copied is Frank Stebbing, the editor of POW WOW, the newspaper written by prisoners of war whose make-shift radios allowed them access to British broadcasts. POW WOW, circulated in Stalag XVII occasionally, often contained more current news of the war than the local Germans were able to obtain.

A Prayer for Mom

Dear God watch over Her for me,
That she may safely guided be.
Help her each lonely hour to bear,
As I would if I were there.

When she is sleeping watch her then,
that fears may not her dreams offend,
Be ever near her through the day,
Let none but goodness come her way.

Sweet faithful Mother who waits for me,
Beyond a wide and spacious sea
Be merciful dear God I pray
Take care of her while I'm away.

Letter to My Wife

I wrote a letter to my darling wife
Saying her husband is well.
For in the prison letter
There wasn't much more I could tell.

I have never forgotten
The look on her loving face.
But this I just couldn't tell her
For I didn't have the space.

I hope she doesn't mind it,
And that she'll forgive me, too
For all I could add in this letter
Was one little "I love you."

A Kriegie's Life

Thirteen barracks in a row
four thousand men sleeping head to toe
plywood and boards, they call a bed
rolled up coats. Hold up your head

two little blankets to keep out the cold
where hundreds of lice hide in each fold
dirty latrines that reek of lime
walks made up of mud and slime

food served us in a dirty pail
bread that's moldy, hard and stale
stoves that have no fuel to burn
dirt that would make your stomach turn

Jerry guards patrol each fence
always alert and on defense
that is the life of an airman will see
when he hits the sack in Germany.

—ROBERT BROOKS
P.O.W. KREMS, AUSTRIA
1944

My Prison Bed

My prison bed is three beds high
    It's also two beds wide
I sleep up in the middle
    With another by my side.

Two more sleep above us
    Thank God there's none below
Because to sleep next to the floor
    Just adds to a prisoner's woe.

The beds are full of fleas and lice
    And I almost forgot the bedbugs
I'd rather sleep on a nice clean floor
    Covered over with rag rugs.

Our springs consist of bedboards
    The mattress made of straw
The blankets are made of a pulpy wood
    Against which there should be a law.

Oh! To sleep on a springy bed
    With sheets of snowy white
Soft wool blankets to cover me
    When I go to sleep at night.

People at home who complain of small things
    Are crazy in the head
And should be made to spend one night
    On my wooden prison bed.

          —"Chic" Ferrino, Stalag XVII B
               Krems, Austria, 1944

Ain't We All in This Bloody Thing Together?

It's the old Army code, boy: we're birds of a feather,
And we share'n share alike, be it win or be it weather
What's yours is mine—and what's mine ain't worth a mention—
Ain't we all in this bloody thing together?
Oh, you don't have to cry when a Johnnie burns your tie
Or a buddy reads your mail—for together we shall die
So open up your parcel and pass around the sweets—
The army don't sit down and watch a man while he eats.
At the post, on the hike, it is share and share alike,
Be it love, be it lead, be it leather
So spill out the box boy—and don't be a pike
Ain't we all in this bloody thing together?
So, you don't wanna share, so you don't think it's fair?
And to hell with the boys—well that's fine—!
But you'll find by and by when it comes turn to die
That death plays no favorites on the line,
For its share—share—share alike there;
and you ain't gonna ask a buddy whether
He is he, and you are you—in that final rendezvous
We'd be all in this bloody thing together,
So it's butts on the chow, and it's butts on the God
and I'm gonna wear your britches out to dine
For it's all an even swap when you've gone over the top
And every man's a buddy on the line.

—FRANK STEBBING
P. O. W. 1944

Christmas Time

Christmas time is coming
Another away from you
And though it's a cheerful season
I can't help feeling blue.

Perhaps I'm sounding bitter,
As I sit and write this rhyme.
But "Darling," how I miss you,
This coming Christmas time.

Here I am a prisoner,
In this land across the sea.
And my thoughts cannot be cheerful,
For you are away from me.

Next year we'll be together
Our dreams will be sublime
But "Darling" how I miss you
This coming "Christmas Time."

—"CHIC" FERRINO
KREMS, AUSTRIA

Prepare for the Fight

Do you tackle the trouble that came your way,
With a resolute heart and a cheerful?
Or, hide your face from the light of day,
With a craven heart and a fearful.
Oh! A trouble's a ton or a trouble's an ounce,

Or a trouble is what you make it.
And it isn't the fact that you're hurt that counts,
But only how did you take it.
You're beaten to earth, well well, what's that?

Come up with a smiling face.
It's nothing against you to fall down flat,
But to life there, that's disgrace.
The harder you're thrown, why, the higher you bounce,
Be proud of your blackened eye.
It isn't the fact that you're licked that counts,
It's how did you fight, and why.
And though you be done to death, what then?
If you battled the best you could;
If you played your part, in the battle of war,
Why, the critics will call it good.
Death comes with a crawl, or it comes with a pounce,
and whether he's slow or spry,
It isn't the fact that you're dead that counts
But only how did you die.

—FRANK STEBBING
P.O.W. 1944

Red Cross Parcel Day

Everyone is feeling good,
They all act sort of gay
You ask me what's the reason?
Why! Today is parcel day.

All week long "Mr. Gloom" prevails,
Gripes and growls hold sway,

Why the cheerful "Puss" on Friday?
Why! Today is parcel day.

Take away their privileges,
you won't hear them complain
But take away their parcels,
That really brings them pain.

They trade d-Bars for C-Rations,
Milk for cigarettes,
And when the trading's over
There are none who have regrets.

Though the prison life is none too good,
they manage day by day.
But I wonder what would happen,
If there were no parcel day.

—"Chic" Ferrino
P.O.W., Krems, Austria

Mamma's Boy

You say he can't stand the army.
The life is too rough—how sad.
Do you think he is any better
Than some other mother's lad?

You have brought him up like a baby
He doesn't smoke or drink—you brag.
If all the others were like him,
What would become of our flag.

You say let the roughnecks do the fighting.
They are used to the beans and the stew.
But, I'm glad that I'm classed with the roughnecks,
That fight for the Red, White, and Blue.

We fly in all kinds of weather,
And come back with a grin on our face
While your darling sits in the parlor
And lets a man fight in his place.

You say his girl couldn't bear to send
Her sweetheart out with the rest.
Do you think she'll feel very proud of him,
When the enemy's breath's on her breast.

You can thank the stars and stripes in Old Glory
'Tis not blurred with any such stain
Because there are ten million roughnecks
That carry red blood in their veins.

You're right, we do smoke, drink, and gamble,
But I fight as our forefathers did
So warm the milk in his bottle
Thank god we don't need your kid.

—Anonymous P.O.W.
Stalag XVII B

You Are Not Alone in Slumber, Buddy, Buddy

a memoriam

I have gathered up the poppies that survived the shearing shell
I have borrowed from Mohammed cactus leaves he would not sell
I have dreamed the desert's beauty from the crippled hills of hell
       And I wear a wreath of sorrow—Buddy, Buddy.

I have scouted mid the embers of the trenches but in vain
I have crawled upon the mountain, along the desert-lane
Seeking but a badge of Jesus to adorn a valiant strain.
       But your crucifix is cactus—Buddy, Buddy.

I have sought among the ruins where the gusts of flags accrue
But I cannot find a fragment of the dear old flag we knew.
To fold upon your mem'ry and to ward the sands from you—
       So I lay you with your buttons—Buddy, Buddy.

I have commandeered a fraction of Africa's old breast.
With my fingers I have torn for you a bivouac of rest.
And your boots are turned to heaven, and your eyes are to the west,
       I have well fulfilled my promise—Buddy, Buddy.

And I cannot bring you bugles as I close your weary eyes
As I clasp your hands together 'neath the blue of foreign skies,
But a part of me detaches and descends to you and dies—
       You are not alone in slumber—Buddy, Buddy.

Overnight Pass

I know on the door of angels
in the faint and starry light
Ma'am a private would like to have
a furlough overnight.

"But you had a pass last evening,"
the lovely Captain said.
"And the night before, and the night before
Don't you like your Army bed?"

"It isn't the quarters, Captain,"
And I see the stars in her eyes,
Blink and softly soften.
"You're homesick, lad," she sighs.

And she takes a scrap of blanket,
And scribbles heavily,
"Here is a pass, now travel fast
And be back before reveille."

So I board the train of slumber
and homeward I am bound.
But I'll be back by the self-same track,
When the bugler breaks the dawn.

—Frank Stebbing
P.O.W.

Prison Window

I'm looking thru the window
of barracks thirty-four
It's the same old dirty window
that I've looked through before.

I see a German "Poster"
standing in the street.
A group of prisoners talking
at a place they chanced to meet.

The wire fence that encircles us
is very plain to see
It holds our bodies prisoners
but our hearts and souls are free

And every man in his talk
mentions the day round the bend,
when all the world lays down its arms
and the war comes to an end.

With hearts full of hope we patiently wait
for that trip across the sea.
It's while looking through the window
that all these things I see.

BY FRANK STEBBING P.O.W.

January 5, 1944:
Foreign food I do not relish
in the best of strangers' houses
in his land a man is better
in his home a man is greater.

Kriegies' Everyday Talk

In his eclectic journal, Carano enjoyed recording witty and profound sayings that he overheard. He jotted down the casual conversation that he heard every day in camp. Slang expressions from the 1940s, acerbic exchanges between American prisoners, and even lines from the dramatic programs performed by the men all found their way into Carano's YMCA book.

When things get too rough for the rest of the world, it will be just right for a "Kriegie."

When the war tremblor ends, and the dust settles, and the actual truth is known, the horrors of it will strike us like a tidal wave.

One soldier to another: "Steve, I'll bet you we don't get out of here before Christmas. I heard from _____."
"Yeah, I know! And only last week you were saying we'd spend the Labor Day Holidays at the 'Catskills.' Charlie, go jump in the shit house!"

A nude soldier trying to rouse a sleeping G.I. "Georgie, Sie Haben Sie Strikholtz?"
"Rouse mit, Ich gay Schlaffen."

A POW speaking to a character in drag on the opposite page: "Hey Lee! I'll bet you two d-bars that you won't come over on this page to sleep tonight."

"Lee," in women's clothing: "That's fine, that's gratitude. Put on a show for you flak happy jerks, and what do we get? Thanks? Hell, no. Propositions. One more crack line like that and off comes this Pollyass Wig."

Krems, Austria, October 1, 1944

As much as actions and incidents, words may be remembered to recall a period of life never to be forgotten. Such are these listed, a bit brazen and harsh perhaps, but it must be remembered, soldiers talk in any army or language is not very pretty speech.

"Deal, for Christ's sake, deal." The Gremlin.

"Throw him into the shit house." The usual answer to a phony story.

"You had it sarge, you had it."

"Haaard luck—tough shit. Whadder you want me to do—punch your ticket?"

"I ain't the chaplain."—in answer to cries of self-pity from a fellow prisoner.

"What stool did that come off of?" answer to a new rumor.

"Why don't you go out and get confiscated?"

"Oh my shattered ass! My achin' back."

"Nix arbict—Gang shlaffen—Fuck roll call." Answer to a German's rouse.

"Vas iss loss here" after Germans announce a number check.

Chow Detail

"Ferrano for barrack chief"—after a speech by same.

Your friend and mine H. E. Moore (song).

"That's no shit, it came straight from the White House." White house is the barrack occupied by our camp leader Kurtenbach and staff.

"Timer" "a group Ten" meaning a German is in the barrack.

"Who's next on the stove?"—cooking time.

"At ease the news" war news about to be read.

"What got you Pal, flak or fighters?" one of the thousands of questions asked a new prisoner.

"That pisses me off "—when someone is aggravated.

"Why did you pull your rip cord?"

"There I was at 20,000 feet," beginning of a story of the gunner's last mission.

"Sie haben sie licht?"—asking for a light.

"Hit the sack before you have an attack."

Ta-wang—gg! Over-raise in a poker game.

The saddest words a man ever said were, "Please deal me out," poker player losing his last chip.

"Get off your dead ass," politely asking a Kriegie to move from your chair or bed.

"The flak was so thick you could get out and walk on it"—gunner's description of a tough mission.

"Close the hangar doors," an appeal by a fellow Kriegie for quiet after lights out at night.

"Dushe" German word for bath.

"Flea-bitten bastard"—pet nickname.

"Get on the shit eatin ball"—meaning hurry up.

"Aw go chin yourself on the warning wire."

"Haben sie ball scratch?" Groth's favorite question.

"Take a bow boy—submerge."

"Dumb shit"—turd head.

"How about a brew?" cup of coffee (Nescafe).

"Abie the mole" nickname for German tunnel searcher.

"They Fly for Dollars"

German propaganda, made readily available in Stalag XVII by the German captors, was designed to undermine the spirit of the Allied soldiers, and Carano included several pieces in his journal. He hand-copied this article from Der Adler, *dated December 14, 1943.*

"THEY FLY FOR DOLLARS"
by war correspondent Hans Theodore Wagner

When two years ago, the U.S. officially entered the war, it appeared to be the only right course and above all the simplest one to land effective support to "volunteering" for the U.S. Air Force by all sorts of solid promises. That is to say, promises of ringing coin. The British had already introduced a system of "premiums" for the flying crews of their air force, and this system was not far exceeded by that of the U.S. To the lure of money was added the childish delight of every American in all things technical. The reaction of the young American is quite as it may be expected. With cool American deliberations, he views the war in east Asia and the war in the equally distant Europe like this—He will have a splendid new profession, he will fly in one of the fantastic "big ships" about which American newspapers relate such wonderful things. He will earn a pot of money and have nothing to worry about—he will not be called up for the land army, nor for the navy, and consequently he will run no risk of being torpedoed by a submarine—an experience which is said to be quite probable and extremely unpleasant.

Furthermore, he will wear a smart new uniform, and then with the help of his flying experience, and the money he has accumulated, he will obtain a particularly good job in the near future in one of the big airline companies. Many of these young Americans, however, have solely the desire to earn money, to adventure around a bit, to have a look at good old Europe. The idea that they may never come back does not seem to worry them. That is a risk that must be taken into account. For flying a bomber in wartime [is] a business like every other one and every business even if it appears to be bomb-proof can of course go wrong.

To meet American and British fliers who are now prisoners of war in Germany is an experience in itself. It is not difficult to find an explanation for the contemptuous attitude of the British flier for his American comrades. When asked how he likes living together with prisoners of war of the U.S. air force, the English flier is usually silent. All the more striking therefore, was the sudden outbreak of the English flying officer who hit the nail on the head when he said, "You as a German fly for your country—I fly for my country—the American flies for money."

It has been repeatedly impressed upon the U.S. pilot that if he is taken prisoner, he must keep silent and answer no questions. That is, of course, a military rule. But, nevertheless, a conversation usually develops, and the replies, the reports, of these young U.S. fliers are striking proofs of their actual attitudes and of the views on their employment as bomber pilots, and of the war in general, from the dangers of which a friendly fate has just saved them.

There is the 22 year old John M. from the state of Alabama. His father had had the lease of a small farm, but, as a result of the American economic system, his family, like hundreds of thousands of others, had failed, despite strenuous and indefatigable labor, to make a success of their venture. In 1935 they packed their few belongings into their Ford and from that time onwards led a gypsy sort of experience. John M. was then fourteen years old. He became an odd-job lad and with seventeen years was lucky enough to get employment in a Ford factory. He later was dismissed and disappeared in the stream of American high road life. Then came the war and with it came John's big chance. He became a gunner in a European bomber group. For the first time in his life he earned a lot of money and led a carefree existence. He made a fresh wide awake impression. The terror of the crash and the parachute jump were forgotten, for him the war was over, and with it another piece of his adventurous life.

Another farmer's son merits our interest—Edward G. from Memphis, Tennessee, 24 years old, the son of a well-to-do farmer from the Mississippi district of the South, a pilot, married for two years. "When I volunteered for the U.S. air force and wanted to go to Europe, Daddy said to me— 'You are right—we must win this war quickly, that's the way to a new prosperity and to make the farm yield a good profit.'" The shrewd farmer's son from Mississippi cherished the dream that after this war, as in the legendary good times after 1918, American agriculture would get bushels of money for its products, for which there would be a great demand everywhere and most especially in the devastated Europe. To the question as to what he had already earned in "premiums," he only laughed and said "business secret."

Another example: George S., 26 years old wireless operator from New York. When he was twenty he started business in the stock exchange. He earned a lot of money and in 1938 even made a trip to Europe. He relates quite freely that big business after the war will be flying. The "American Air Lines" will embrace the whole world. We have now entered a new "Icarus" era. One must take advantage of this chance. For this, one needs flying experience, one must be familiar with the object. When the war is over, I shall easily manage to switch myself into this big business. In addition, I have had my experience as a bomber pilot. At this George laughed and seemed to enjoy his own cleverness.

Another man was furious that he had been shot down. First of all he swore hard and then he related that he only needed one more bombing raid in order to be able to buy himself a certain little inn on the upper Hudson. This man, 23 years old, Richard B., also from New York, once a dishwasher, then an ice cream vendor, and finally a dock laborer, behaved so atrociously towards his British comrades that he came within an ace of being beaten up by them. The way of these young fliers from their entry into the air force to their being shot down is nearly always the same. On the completion of their training they are allotted to a group and begin their European operations with the transatlantic flight to England.

The successful flight, the admiration of the British people for their splendid "flying ships" give them a tremendous confidence in their own weapon. British propaganda conjures up for them a fairly misleading picture of the air defense. Not until they reach the British aeries do they gradually acquire a true-to-life picture of the air situation, especially when as occasionally happens—whole squadrons fail to return from their flying operations.

Night raids are always flown by the British bomber formations. They become increasingly difficult, owing to the German strength of the growing air defense. Daylights are reserved for the U.S. formations. We shall let a U.S. pilot narrate his own experience during his last bombing raid over Germany. The pilot Foran D.—from Chicago, 27 years old, and a sergeant, relates, "We couldn't get out of range of the German air defense, one fresh squadron after another of fighters and destroyers swooped in to attack us. The co-operation between the flak and fighters was excellent, they gave us hell from above and below. We lost one engine after another. The end came quickly for us. The majority of my crew were mortally wounded when our bus suddenly moved downwards. How I got out of it, I don't know. Instinctively, I pulled the rip cord. I was lucky I guess. I am the only survivor of my squadron. At any rate, I haven't seen a single one of my comrades in any of the German prisoner of war camps."

These utterances of captured U.S. pilots will suffice. We know what we are to think of our opponents. That the strength of our defense is increasing and that it tackles the Anglo-American terrorist fliers with growing ferocity is a fact that cannot be withheld from the American public. The "business" of "terrorist flying" will cost them dearly, both the big business jobbers, and the little ones who entrust themselves to the flying ships—that is to say—the "flying coffins."

About the War

On occasion, as Carano notes, Allied propaganda found its way into the camp, escaping the German's notice.

Everything that comes into a Kriegie camp is censored with hawk-eye scrutiny, principally reading material—however the following story apparently missed the censor's eye.

Let us never forget what the Germans do when they have power. Let us look at France and remember one stroke of the invader's authority. The whole world knows the French working men are being recruited and sent to Germany to work in factories and farms. A great many naïve people are under the delusion not only that the French workmen make the migration willingly, but that the employment of foreign labor in German industry is a temporary measure, a device of war, and when peace is made the Frenchman can go back to France, and the Germans will do the work in Germany.

To call this child-like faith, naïve, is to dignify it, because there is in naïveté a kind of innocent beauty, but this [in]stead, is credulity of a very dangerous sort. Let the Germans themselves dispel the illusion. The *Parises Zeitgung,* a German newspaper published in Paris, recently announced that the German occupation authorities have determined upon a radical revision of the French children's educational system. French children, says the newspaper, need no general schooling as they will have no need for education later in life. Under the new system, it goes on to say the children will have a brief term at school and then be apprenticed in industry to provide the skilled workers Germany needs. This system, the paper cold-bloodedly remarks, provides increasing numbers of French workers for German units. This means enslavement of body-mind, and spirit. This means that a generation of children will be bred to work as living machines, contented not to know, and not to hope. And this fate is prepared too, for Belgians, Czechs, Slovaks, and Poles.

We must be very sure that in those legions of the enslaved there will not be wanted also the Americans. For it is the Americans who will bring them liberation with "Victory."

Liberation Account

*Toward the end of his journal, Carano drew the out-
lines of his buddies' dog-tags and wrote in their names
and addresses of their homes back in the States. Those
last pages served as a recording of the fraternity that they
had formed, even a promise to resume their friendships
after their normal lives had been restored after the war.
An addendix lists their names, along with the addresses
they gave Carano in 1944.*

*On a loose page tucked into the end-flaps of his jour-
nal, Staff Sergeant Carano kept notes after the liberation
of Stalag XVII. What follows are his experiences from
April 8 to May 6, 1945, on the march from Stalag XVII
to liberation by American troops in Branau on the border of Austria and Germany. The first page of Carano's
notes is unfortunately missing.*

. . . after about five days marching none of us really expected anything to happen to get us back to the U.S. after passing so many places
where we saw atrocities.

We had begun to think it was just a matter of time until they got us
to a place where they would eliminate us. Several times as we passed
through a village we would come across units of the German Volkstrum.
Though we were warned many times by our guards against antagonizing
them, several times we would have to be rushed through a village for fear
of an uprising among them because of their ages. Ranging from seven to
seventy, they were pretty "dangerous," and G.I.s, though warned, were
continuously teasing them with names like Pop, Squirt, etc.

The march took us through towns, villages, up hills, through valleys. On almost all the large hills or mountains could be seen German defenses and road blocks. Many places along a road that had been cut on the side of a mountain would be what seemed to be large wooden fences with tons and tons of rocks piled behind them, leverage devices which could be sprung at the touch of a finger, causing half the mountainside to come tumbling down on the road. Every time we passed places like these, we thought for sure some German would release the damn thing on us.

The nights we spent out in the fields were something which today is impossible to believe. With little or no protection against the cold we would huddle in fours and fives to keep warm.

Yet most of us would still be able to kid the German guards who marveled at the improvised leantos, less than a half hour after we reached any field where the Germans would say we were going to spend the night. You couldn't even find a blade of grass which could be used for a fire to keep warm or heat whatever food we might have gotten during the day. Places that we had passed through reminded one of a hoard of locusts in those "before and after" scenes you'd see at a movie.

One night they stopped us near an enormous farm and though the farmer had been warned beforehand that we would stop there, in the morning his barn, fields, and even his house had been broken into. I managed to get into the basement where he kept meat and stuff so for one night about ten of us in our group had what might be considered a feast. That same night Culver and I slept in the farmer's house on a bed, the likes of which I've never seen in my life. As I've said, I had learned to speak German pretty well so that almost every place we had been, I managed pretty well to get us some clothing or food. This night was a triumph. I got Hans the guard to let me talk to the farmer and his wife. After about ten minutes of some pretty sloppy German, Cul and I were in this room. It was spotless and there was a bath, though we must have felt pretty guilty at the time with all the others in the barn in the fields, or wherever they could find a place to bed down. We didn't much give a damn.

We bathed and then sank into a bed which was just a large box with a mattress made of feathers about three feet thick. It was so warm and comfortable that it took us at least three hours to fall asleep. In the morning when we awoke, everybody was gone. The farmer and wife begged us to stay, but after thanking them and having a breakfast of eggs, white bread, and coffee, we left them and with rushing all the way, caught up with the rear column after about two hours.

Letter from Dutch Nurses

After the war ended, the Dutch nurses who tended Carano during his recuperation found his address in Brooklyn and wrote the postcard below, dated August 30, 1945. Clearly he made a favorable impression on them when he was their patient.

Dear Mr. Carano,

We hope you got home safely by now. Did you have a bad time in the camp? Over here, the last time it was very bad, but we got over it and we are very happy to be free and all the war is over!

We hope you remember us, we were the Dutch nurses from the operating room. We always had great fun in being just a bit cleverer than the Germans who watched us with suspicious eyes, and giving you the latest news.

If you can find the time, please let us know how you did get on in the camp and reached home.

Yours sincerely,
E. Gerda, Erna Finch, Nellie Kluger
Amsterdam

Appendix

Carano's Barrack Comrades in Stalag XVII B

Joseph Balesh
507—West 5th St.
Brooklyn, New York

Charles F. Bang
1400 S. Edgewood St.
Arlington, Virginia, Apt. 536

Homer L. Boyette
2064 N. Jones St.
Winnfield, Louisiana

Marshall F. Bryan
Thornhill Heights
Frankfort, Kentucky

Clyde T. Bush
Belle Fourche
South Dakota

Paul M. Caveny
1112 N. 2nd St.
Springfield, Illinois

Roger Christensen
Marne, Iowa
Shot down Dec. 1, 1943

Roland Conners
1164 Parsons Ave.
Columbus, Ohio

R. E. Crawford
48 N. Evergreen Ave.
Youngstown, Ohio

Richard Cuirezak
2480 Mackenna Aven.
Niagara Falls, New York

Charles J. Culver
Route 1, Henderson, Kentucky
Shot down Dec. 1, 1943
Leverkus, Germany
(Right waist gunner)

Charles Cummings
Box Route 3
Hillsboro, Texas

James W. Deese
256 2nd St.
Macon, Georgia

Jim Dixon
1700 Outer Street, Joe Ave.
Evansville, Indiana

Gilly Dobrinski
4126 North 24th St.
Milwaukee, Wisconsin

Wallace Emmert
Route 3, Box 23
Madera, California

William P. England
Box 42
Des Moines, New Mexico
Shot down Dec. 1, 1943
Leverkus, Germany (engineer)

Walter Ferrens
165 East 13th St.
Oswego, New York

Quentin E. Freed
705 William St.
Youngstown, Ohio

Charles C. Gattman
P.O. Box 928
El Paso, Texas

William R. Gennette
3220 Whiteney Ave.
Detroit, Michigan

Rodo Giuseppe
Pentedattilo
Beggio C.

Edward H. Gracey
2229 Algard St.
Philadelphia, Pennsylvania

Charles Groth
1171—72nd St.
Brooklyn, New York
Schweinfurt Oct. 14, 1943

Joseph E. Hafer
2207 Taliafero St.
Tampa, Florida

Harry A. Hall
2434 E. 16th St.
Oakland, California

Michael R. Henneberg
Mt. Vernon Post Office
New York

Fredrick Holt
81 Bowling Land
Bradford, Rhode Island

Coolidge Howlett
Box 413
Jackson, Kentucky

Johnnie N. Johnson
5000 Bryant
Kansas City, Missouri

Carlton A. Josephson
8 Superior Avenue
Newington, Connecticut
Shot down Dec. 1, 1943,
Leverkus, Germany (Engineer)

Floyd J. Karns
29 Musening St.
Oil City, Pennsylvania

Robert Kelly
30 Greenwood Road
Sharon Hill, Pennsylvania

George W. King
10 Battles St.
Brockton, Massachusetts

William H. Kithcart
57 Webster Ave.
Patterson, New Jersey

Joe E. Lassiter "Slim" 6'7"
5344 Rock Ave.
Chicago, Illinois

Herbert A. Lee
35 Beach St.
Stapelton, Long Island

William E. Make
711—8th Ave.
Aberdeen, Washington

Anthony Mauceri
1399 Greene Ave.
Brooklyn, New York

John McKenna
168 Eastman Ave.
Rochester, New York

Gerald Minch
Route 2
Plymouth, Wisconsin

Russell H. Mowan
243 ? N. Main St.
Mansfield, Ohio

William C. Nichols
1328 S. First St.
Louisville, Kentucky

Howard Parks
8721 N. Edison
Portland, Oregon

Carl Peters
1317 Rhode Island Ave.
Washington, D.C.

John H. Riaaw
279 Prospect Ave.
Orange, New Jersey

Floyd G. Riddle
Blue Ridge, Texas

Robert R. Roeder
Friedensburg, Pennsylvania

Raymond P. Sanford
2016 S. Sierra Vista Ave.
Alhambra, California

John J. Schnalzer
255 Franklin St. S.E.
Warren, Ohio

Bob Schock
409 Willow Avenue
Altoona, Pennsylvania

Paul Schwarz
1820—15th St.
Sacramento, California

Gordon H. Shields
14 Russell St.
Hudson Falls, New York

Joseph A. Sieber
1829 N. Castle St.
Baltimore, Maryland

Sherman W. Sly
Route 1
Yonkers, Oklahoma

Bernard E. Snow
P.O. Box 472
Carpenteria, California

George A. Stuart
1904 Belknap St.
Superior, Wisconsin

James A. Watkins
714 North Race St.
Princeton, Indiana

Carano, third from left in the rear, was photographed with his fellow crew members in Texas before they shipped out to England in the fall of 1943. Beside him, fourth from left, is eighteen-year-old Bill Blackmon, with his arm around Carano's shoulders. *Courtesy of Stephen F. Carano.*

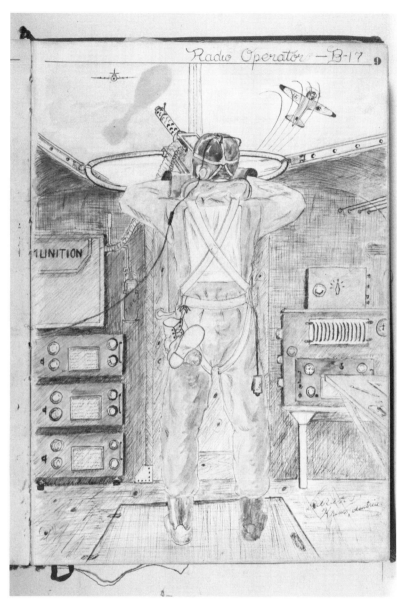

In his only self portrait, Carano drew himself in action firing at Nazi planes. Though he drew his fellow POWs' faces in Stalag XVII B, he chose to draw himself while fighting the enemy. Illustration by Claudio Stefano Carano. *Courtesy of Stephen F. Carano.*

A WARTIME LOG

A REMEMBRANCE
FROM HOME
THROUGH THE AMERICAN Y.M.C.A.

Published by
THE WAR PRISONERS' AID OF THE Y. M. C. A.
37 Quai Wilson
GENEVA — SWITZERLAND

Front page of Carano's Wartime Log journal. The books were produced by the YMCA and distributed by the Red Cross to prison camps throughout Europe with instructions for POWs to use them in any way they wished. Among the suggestions were letters they might want to send home but knew would be censored, records of everyday life, poetry and drawings. Illustration by Claudio Stefano Carano. *Courtesy of Stephen F. Carano.*

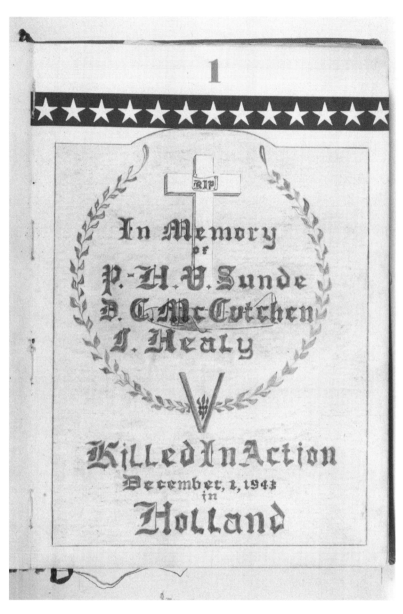

On one of the first pages in Carano's journal he drew a memorial to the three killed, Sunde, McCutchon, and Healy, when their plane crashed on a bombing mission over Germany. Illustration by Claudio Stefano Carano. *Courtesy of Stephen F. Carano.*

Rose CARANO 1971 W.10th ST. BK 331.

Darling   Nov. 19th 1944

This letter may never reach you, for no one knows what the outcome of this war will be, or what may befall the bearer, as I am entrusting it to a very dear friend, who I am sure will do his utmost to deliver it, his name is Charles Groth, and if any thing should happen to me I know he can tell you all you would like to know about myself and the way we have lived in this hole, in this way only can you know why, I and Josephson, & Bang are attempting this escape. One year in a German prison camp is just one year too long to be away from the ones I love especially yourself and my son who is growing rapidly and forgetting (if ever he knew,) that his father really existed. Something just had to be done and as you my wife know how long I can possibly be tied down in one place especially being away from you, Stevie, Mom, & Dad.

I somehow feel that if I didn't at least try to get home before these damned Germans decide to quit, I don't feel that I could ever again feel as though I was half the man I ever considered myself. If anything should happen to me and my two Buddies, I want you to know that it is for the love of the ones at home that we are trying our best to go to them as quickly as possible. I always have and always will love you all.

In November 1944, Carano decided to escape from Stalag XVII B, along with two of his comrades, Carlton Josephson and Charles Bang. He wrote this secret letter to his wife, Rose, and gave it to Charles Groth, a fellow Brooklynite, for safekeeping. *Courtesy of Stephen F. Carano.*

Carlton Arthur Josephson
95 Shuttle Meadow Avenue
New Britain Conn.

Charles F. Bang
apt. 536 – 1400 S. edgewood sT.
Arlington Va.

For Charlie Groth only
Please do not read

Claudio Carano

On the back of his escape letter, Carano carefully wrote the addresses of Josephson and Bang in case they didn't succeed in their escape. *Courtesy of Stephen F. Carano.*

Portrait of Kenneth J. "Kurt" Kurtenbach, elected the "Man of Confidence" by the inmates in Stalag XVII B. Carano captures Kurtenbach's strong leadership and determination. Illustration by Claudio Stefano Carano. *Courtesy of Stephen F. Carano.*

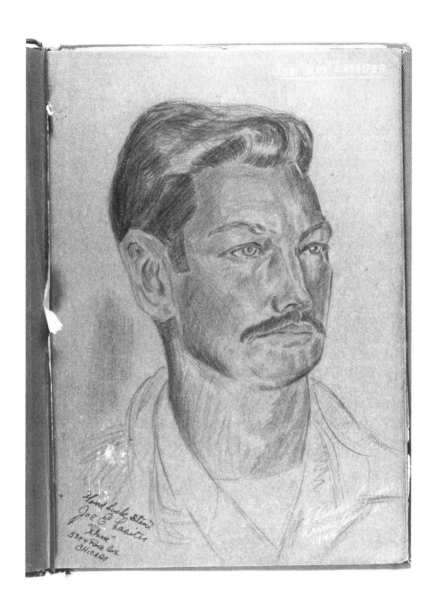

Portrait of Joseph "Slim" Lassiter. Carano remarked upon Lassiter's "piercing eyes that see much but show little, [and his] silence of manner that commands respect without force." Illustration by Claudio Stefano Carano. *Courtesy of Stephen F. Carano.*

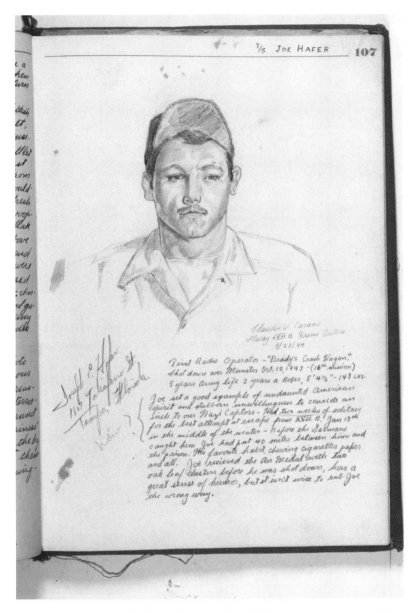

Claudio J Carano
Stalag XVII B Krems Austria
9/27/44

First Radio Operator - "Brady's Crash Wagon".
Shot down over Munster Oct. 10, 1943 - (16th mission)
5 years Army life 2 years a Boxer, 5' 4½" - 148 LBS.

Joseph P. Hafer
1500 Talismiore St.
Tampa, Florida

Joe set a good example of undaunted American
spirit and stubborn unwillingness to concede an
inch to our Nazi Captors- Had two weeks of solitary
for the best attempt at escape from XVII B. Jan 18th
in the middle of the winter - before the Germans
caught him Joe had put 40 miles between him and
the prison. His favorite habit, chewing cigarettes paper
and all. Joe recieved the Air Medal with two
oak leaf clusters before he was shot down, has a
great sense of humor, but it isn't wise to rub Joe
the wrong way.

Portrait of Joseph Hafer, in which Carano testifies to his "best attempt at escape" from Stalag XVII B, when Hafer was forty miles away before the Germans caught him. Illustration by Claudio Stefano Carano. *Courtesy of Stephen F. Carano.*

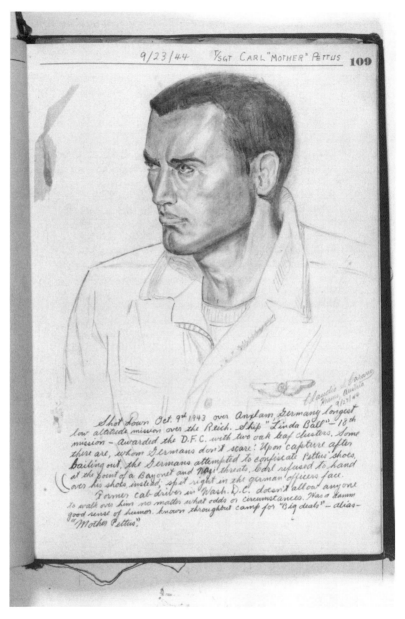

Portrait of Carl Pettus, who won his comrades' admiration for spitting in the face of the German who demanded his shoes after he was captured. Illustration by Claudio Stefano Carano. *Courtesy of Stephen F. Carano.*

Portrait of Charles Groth. Bill Blackmon recalled that Carano and Groth, "two hard-headed guys from Brooklyn," frequently got into shouting matches, "and then it would be gone. They'd be arm in arm, walking down the street, best buddies." It was to Groth that Carano entrusted his escape letter to his wife, Rose. Illustration by Claudio Stefano Carano. *Courtesy of Stephen F. Carano.*

German flak over Cologne devastated the B-17, turning the waist "into a horrible confusion of blood and debris." Flak injured every crew member in the waist of the bomber. Illustration by Claudio Stefano Carano. *Courtesy of Stephen F. Carano.*

POWs passed the time counting the barbs in the wire fence around the camp. Carano wrote that "'The Wire' is at the end of every road, blocking every dream, every plan, every vain soaring of your enthusiasm . . . at dusk it frames the western sun in a black spider web of prickly steel. Even the sun is captive." Illustration by Claudio Stefano Carano. *Courtesy of Stephen F. Carano.*

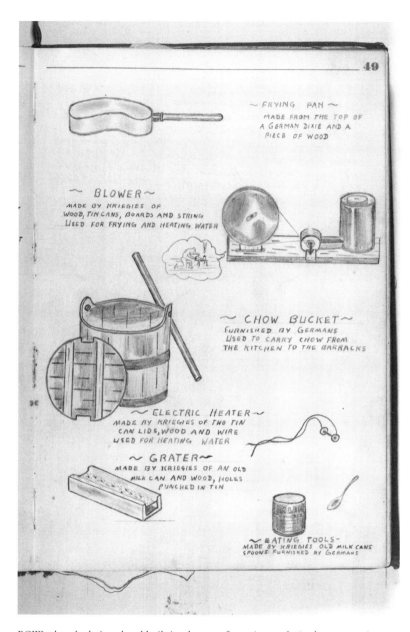

POWs cleverly designed and built implements for various tasks in the camp, using whatever items they could find. Bill Blackmon remembers that Carano and other men constructed their own wireless radios, which, when working well, could bring them precious news of the war from Great Britain. Illustration by Claudio Stefano Carano. *Courtesy of Stephen F. Carano.*

~ BROOM ~
FURNISHED BY GERMANS
MADE OF A BUNDLE OF TWIGS

~ BUTTER BURNER ~
MADE BY KRIEGIES OF AN
OLD SALMON CAN BUTTER
AND CLOTH WICK
USED TO FURNISH LIGHT

~ DRINKING CUP ~
MADE BY KRIEGIES OF A USED
BUTTER CAN, STEEL BAND AND WOOD

~ STOOL ~
FURNISHED BY GERMANS
VERY HARD TO FIND ONE
NOT IN USE

~ PLUNGER ~
MADE BY KRIEGIES OF BUTTER
CAN, LIVER PATE CAN AND HANDLE
USED FOR WASHING CLOTHES

Illustration by Claudio Stefano Carano. *Courtesy of Stephen F. Carano.*

Bela-Clava (gray)
(German)

English Army cap (brown)

French Army Cap

American "G.I." knit cap (brown)

Hand-made Cap
(blue & gray scarf and cardboard)

Winter Hood — blue scarf
heated suit zipper (hand made)

Headgear provided not only warmth during the brutally harsh Austrian winters, but also a sense of identity and creativity. Illustration by Claudio Stefano Carano. *Courtesy of Stephen F. Carano.*

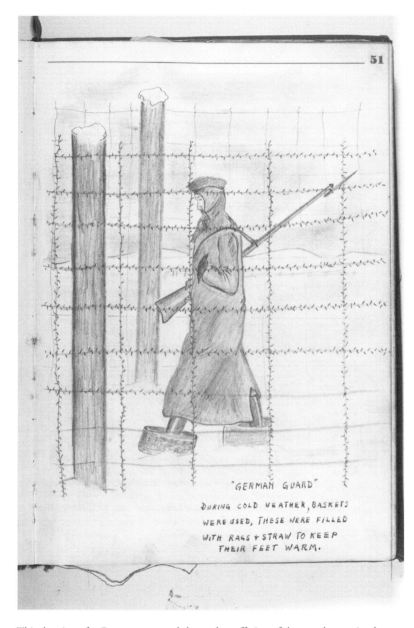

"GERMAN GUARD"

DURING COLD WEATHER, BASKETS
WERE USED, THESE WERE FILLED
WITH RAGS + STRAW TO KEEP
THEIR FEET WARM.

This drawing of a German on patrol shows the suffering of the guards, wearing baskets on their feet to serve as a kind of snow shoe, stuffed with straw for warmth. Illustration by Claudio Stefano Carano. *Courtesy of Stephen F. Carano.*

ITALIAN PRISONERS, BETTER KNOWN TO KRIEGIES AS "FREE MEN". THIS NICKNAME WAS
ATTACHED TO THEM WHEN AN ARTICLE IN A GERMAN PAPER STATED THAT ALL
ITALIAN PRISONERS OF WAR WERE TO BE SET FREE (THEY NEVER HAVE BEEN)

RUSSIAN AND SERB WOMEN WERE PUT
TO WORK HARVESTING WHEAT AND OTHER
CROPS IN GERMANY AND OCCUPYING COUNTRIES.

Without the protection of the Geneva Convention, Russians and Italians received terrible abuse at the hands of their captors. Carano observed, "In every city, town and village in German-controlled Europe, Russian slaves were used to do dirty hard work. Russian men, women and children from conquered territories were brought to Germany by the trainloads." Illustration by Claudio Stefano Carano. *Courtesy of Stephen F. Carano.*

In an abandoned barrack, POWs built a chapel using crates from Red Cross deliveries. The small church was only one part of a functioning community they created, along with a bartering system, entertainment, and negotiating process with the Germans through the election of their Man of Confidence. Illustration by Claudio Stefano Carano. *Courtesy of Stephen F. Carano.*

76

Carano's cartoons parodied prison life. In the top left corner, Carano drew himself responding to rumors about the war's end. Below, a POW asks for a light but is rebuffed with the words "Go away, I'm going to sleep." Across the two pages, a POW with chocolate bars attempts to bribe a cross-dressing prisoner named "Lee" to spend

the night. ("Lee" was an Australian POW who replaced the real Lee C. Gordon, a successful escapee from the camp. "Lee" performed in the camp's drag shows to great acclaim.) To the far right, a dignified POW ignores the shenanigans of his fellow inmates.

Cartoons offered comic relief to the tedium of prison days. Here, a POW washes his clothes with one of the "plungers" invented in the prison while he entertains sexual fantasies. Illustration by Claudio Stefano Carano. *Courtesy of Stephen F. Carano.*

Carano's rendition of a German punctures the self-importance of some of the guards. In laughter, the POWs found a source of power and camaraderie. Illustration by Claudio Stefano Carano. *Courtesy of Stephen F. Carano.*

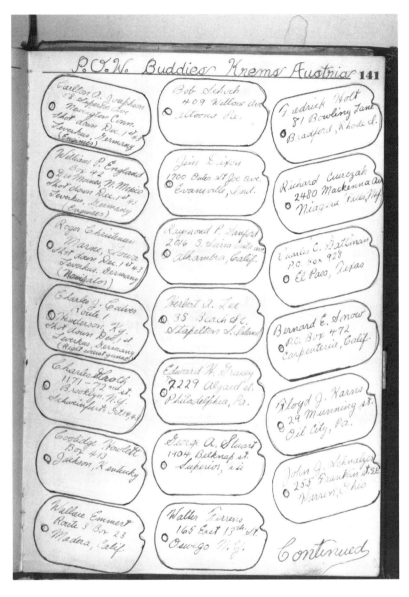

At the end of his journal, Carano meticulously traced in the dogtags of the men in his barracks, penning in their addresses and any other information he had obtained about them. *Courtesy of Stephen F. Carano.*

In 2006, the citizens of Wissous, France, held their annual memorial service for the ten American crewmen whose B-17 crashed near the town as terrified villagers watched on February 6, 1944. The editor, Kay Sloan, lays flowers at the site where her uncle, Tech Sergeant William F. Davidge, was shot down and captured by the Germans. Beside her is her daughter, Signe Schloss. In the background is Pierett Rembur (in coat and pink hat), the French organizer of the event. Fifth from the right is John C. Bitzer, in dark cap, who was a turret gunner in a B-17 shot down in the winter of 1944 near Paris. His wife, Marian, stands beside him to the right. Credit: *La Gazette de Wissous. Courtesy of Kay Sloan.*

2

PART TWO

JOHN C.
BITZER'S
WARTIME LOG

Introduction

With the image of himself and his buddy, "Cul," rushing to catch up with their comrades on the march to liberation, Steve Carano stopped writing in his journal. He tucked away the book, sewn carefully in the durable brown cloth from his Army uniform, and with liberation looming ahead on the German border, he began to live in the present moment again. With freedom fast approaching, and the thrill of fresh eggs for breakfast and feather beds at night, he didn't need to return to those pages that reminded him of his long months in Stalag XVII.

At about the same time that Carano closed the covers of his journal and shut away his wartime past, another young soldier by the name of John C. Bitzer pulled out his own YMCA book, which already contained seven poems and several drawings he had made throughout his months of incarceration in Stalag Luft VI in East Prussia and, later, Stalag Luft IV near Belgard. With his comrades from Stalag Luft IV, he had just completed a torturous six-hundred-mile "death march" across Germany through snow and sub-freezing temperatures, a brutally cold trek that had begun nearly three months before, in early February. For John Bitzer, it was liberation—not the months of trauma or deadly boredom—that inspired him to write entries in his journal. The gnawing uncertainty about the future that had hung over him and his comrades in German prison camps had finally ended. He pulled out a pen to capture the overwhelming relief and joy of the moment for which he, Carano, and countless other prisoners of war had long awaited—the arrival of fellow GIs to bring him back home.

Despite the exhaustion and starvation he'd endured on the death march, Bitzer recorded the elation during those first days in which he and his comrades celebrated their freedom. Like Carano, Bitzer had been a prisoner of war since December 30, 1943, when his plane went down over Germany. Like Carano, he also received a YMCA Log Book, but—until liberation—he had put it to use for poetry, occasional drawings and, most important, the home addresses of his comrades.

Bitzer wrote what he knew he would want to remember. For four days following liberation, he recorded the luxury of having clean clothes, good meals—and the exhilaration of freedom. For Bitzer, at the end of his terrible ordeal, the blank pages of his journal offered a way of personally documenting the grand historic moment of liberation.

At age nineteen, John Bitzer left his hometown of Euclid, Ohio, and enrolled in the U.S. Army Air Force on December 7, 1942. The Army sent him to gunnery school and airplane mechanics training before assigning him to the 447th bomb group, 711 bomb squadron in August 1943. A stocky, broad-shouldered young man, he became a ball turret gunner on a B-17 bomber. The ball turret, located in the belly of the bomber, isolated the man inside from the rest of the ten-man crew, confining him to quarters so cramped that a soldier could not even wear his parachute while operating the gun. It was not a place for claustrophobics. As Bitzer tells it, "To enter the turret it must be rotated until the door opening faces the inside of the plane, this means that the guns will first be pointed to the rear then 90 degrees straight down. Once inside the ball and the hatch shut and latched, the gunner sits curled up in the fetal position, swiveling the entire turret as he aims the two guns. You sit between the guns with feet in stirrups positioned on either side of the thirteen-inch diameter window in the front. One foot operates the gun sight, the other foot operates the intercom. This is why there are no six foot tall turret gunners."

On December 30, 1943, Bitzer was in East Angola, England, with thousands of other American airmen, all making the potentially deadly daytime raids over Nazi-held western Europe. That morning, Bitzer's mission was to bomb the chemical factory at Ludwisghaven, Germany. The flight in was as ordinary as such a mission could ever be: a little flak, minimal fighter action. They successfully dropped the bomb and headed home in formation. With Paris just below them, the bomber was suddenly under attack. Flak knocked out two engines and the B-17 fell out of formation. Soon after, a German MC 110 twin-engine fighter roared up to finish the job on the damaged plane.

Inside the ball turret, Bitzer realized with a sinking feeling that the power to operate the turret was gone. He was locked inside a turret that refused to turn to the exit, the only escape he had from the steel enclosure. "What the hell do I do now?" he remembers thinking, struggling not to panic. In a rush, his training in the States returned: he connected two cranks just above his head and manually jerked them until the turret had rotated in alignment with the exit position. Once out, he saw the radio operator slumped dead, in the center of the plane while a fire raged in the bomb bay. Flak penetrated the shell of the devastated plane and struck Bitzer's right leg while he reached for his parachute. The tail gunner and both waist gunners were already poised to jump. Bitzer said, "I snapped on my chute and went to the waist hatch exit. I was the last to leave just as the plane exploded. The last thing I remember is pulling my rip cord."

Riddled with flak that he still carries in his body, Bitzer woke in a German hospital in Beauveau, France, with a new identity. He was now POW 817. After he sufficiently healed, the Germans sent him to Frankfurt, where the German Air Force had their interrogation center. For five days, he was held in solitary confinement and questioned until he was shipped out by boxcar to a camp near Memel in East Prussia, one of the first group of eighty Americans to open a new compound at Stalag Luft VI. In an understatement, he remembers those Prussian winter days as "mighty cold weather."

At Stalag VI, Bitzer remembers that "the Red Cross parcels saved the day." The contents of each precious, life-saving parcel were embedded in his memory:

> one pound of Klim (powdered milk)
> one pound of margarine
> one can of Spam
> one box of C-ration biscuits
> one pound of raisins
> eight ounces of chocolate
> five packs of cigarettes
> two bars of soap

Though each prisoner was to receive one parcel a week, Bitzer recalls that, in the very best of times, there was one parcel to every two men. Later, four men had to split a parcel.

During his stay in Stalag VI, Bitzer received a Log Book and began to inscribe poetry and drawings in its pages.

As the Russian front advanced across Germany, the prisoners in Stalag VI—all three to four thousand of them—were evacuated in July 1944, and, like his comrades, Bitzer stuffed his few possessions into a small duffel bag, making sure his journal was protected. "I wasn't about to leave it behind," he said. "It was close to my heart for a long time—and it had addresses I'd picked up from the guys, things I didn't want to lose." Once again, the men were crammed into boxcars, stifling in the summer heat this time. The train chugged to the Baltic Sea where, as Bitzer put it in an ironic understatement, "the Baltic Cruise was about to begin." Stepping from the boxcars out into daylight, the prisoners were greeted by the sight of a rusty old tramp steamer at the dock. Here one of the most miserable incidents of his imprisonment thus far occurred, the first of several war crimes he survived. Thousands of POWs disappeared down the narrow hatch into the dark hold below, jammed inside with barely room to stand, barely air to breathe in the suffocating stench. For three days, the only provision offered by the Germans was a solitary bucket in which the POWs could relieve themselves. The bucket was hauled up when it was full of excrement and then lowered back down. Down in the crowded hold there was no food or water and no idea of when the torment would end.

After three days, the hold slid open not to the familiar bucket, but to the sound of German soldiers: "Raus! Raus!" The top of the ladder meant fresh air and light, and another trip on a boxcar. In Bitzer's words, "They took our shoes and belts and handcuffed two of us together. After twenty four hours of travel, we stopped. We got our shoes and belts back but remained handcuffed. The Heydekrug Run was about to begin. Egged on by a mad man, the captain of the guards, we were urged to move things along by bayonet stabs and dog bites. We ran up a hill and through a forest. We never stopped running for three to four kilometers. Machine gun nests were strategically placed in the woods in the event of an attempt to escape. Word came down the line that if you could no longer run and were exhausted to fall by the wayside with your partner and lie still. After reaching camp, we lay exhausted in the Vorlager [the main area around the central warehouse] with no food, water or medical attention. Later a truck went out to pick up those that had fallen by the wayside. They finally brought us some water and soup the next day. We entered our compound and were searched. We had no idea what they were looking for, but we felt it was mostly to make you more miserable. We settled into Stalag Luft IV, Lager D. It was the same story; lousy food and the Red Cross parcels saved the day."

After several months in Stalag IV, the Russian advance once again sent the POWs on the move. Though he seldom used his journal until liberation, later in life he realized the importance of relaying the full historical experience he had undergone. The story is best told in Bitzer's own words, in a speech he delivered to a Rotary Club meeting in Cleveland, Ohio in October, 2004.

Liberation from the Nazis

This was the beginning of the German version of the [Bataan] Death March. On February 6th, 1945, POWs set out on foot. No one knows for sure, but they probably numbered about six thousand. German guards divided the POWs into groups of two hundred fifty or three hundred men, not all of whom traveled the same route or at the same pace. We were told this march would only last three days. Ha! During the day, prisoners marched four to five abreast and at night, if we were lucky, we slept in a barn. Many times we slept in woods or an open field. Germans provided little food and we scrounged for our own food. We often found no more than a potato or a kohlrabi and ate it raw. On occasion Red Cross parcels arrived and we traded cigarettes and other items to guards and civilians for food. We even resorted to stealing the feed that had been thrown to pigs. A handful of stolen grain, eaten while marching, provided a meal.

Adding to the misery, this was one of Germany's coldest winters on record. Snow piled knee deep at times and temperatures went well below zero. Virtually all marchers grew weak. Every POW became infected with lice. Other illnesses also existed such as pneumonia, diphtheria, pellagra, typhus, trench-foot or tuberculosis. The biggest medical problem was dysentery often acquired by drinking contaminated water. Blisters, abscesses and frost bite became epidemic. Medical care was essentially non-existent.

Eventually the long-awaited liberation came in various ways. Some GIs escaped and hid out until they could find an Allied unit. Other POWs had the misfortune to be liberated by the Russians which meant additional confinement at Soviet hands. Most of the POWs were liberated by American or British forces and the hideous march was over.

From beginning to end, the march spanned eighty-six days and

[an] estimated six hundred miles in length. Many survivors went from one hundred fifty pounds to perhaps ninety pounds and suffered injuries and illnesses that plagued them their entire lives. Worst of all, several hundred American soldiers, possibly as many as thirteen hundred, died on this pointless pilgrimage to nowhere.

The "Baltic Cruise," the "Heydekrug Run" and the "Death March" were considered war crimes and recorded as such.

We were liberated April 28, 1945 at Bitterfeld, Germany and that's when I found out what happened to the rest of my crew. The pilot, navigator, radio operator and bombardier were killed. The tail gunner was picked up by the French underground and got back to England. The co-pilot, engineer, two waist gunners and myself became POWs. I got home in June, 1945 on Father's Day and was discharged from the Army in October.

I resumed life as did millions of others after the war. For many years the veterans did not want to talk much about their experiences. You would occasionally read stories now and then.

In the 1980s the National ex-POW Convention was held in Cleveland. I did not wish to attend but my wife suggested otherwise. We went and I was glad I listened to her. We had a side reunion of those Kreigies from Stalag Luft VI and IV. Each man went to the microphone to introduce himself. I could not believe my ears when I heard the name John Monks. I looked up and there was the Kreigie who was my buddy and who I had been handcuffed to through the Heidekrug Run. It was a very emotional meeting and many tears were shed.

The number of World War II veterans is dwindling rapidly. In order for the younger generation to know what happened we must speak out now.

John Bitzer's Wartime Log

LIBERATION
APRIL 26, 1945
6:45 P.M.

After being on the march for two and a half months, since February 6, 1945, we marched into Bitterfeld as free men and as I write this I am sitting in a German office in Bitterfeld—minus the Jerries of course. We left Gross Tyschow Pomerania on the 6th of February and marched to Stalag XI A at Altengrable by Magdeburg. We evacuated XI A because [the Germans knew] the Yanks were getting too close. Incidentally, the Russians were chasing us up till then. From there we came down towards Leigzig to Annaberg; there the Russians chased us again. We finally stayed at a farm and it was rumored we would wait there till the Yanks took us. We could hardly believe that and we didn't. We left there again because Jerry didn't want to be taken by the Russians. Seeing their position, I can't blame them.

Finally the great day came. We left this place and marched to Bitterfeld where we disarmed the Jerries. We shook hands with the first G.I. at 2:45, marched further and saluted the first officer at 3:20. We bummed our first cigarette at 3:45. This has been a great day for all of us and a long awaited day for myself. It's been seventeen months. To be a free man once again is hard to believe. The town here is ours. We can have what we want. We got our K ration supper tonight. K rations has been on our lips for the past week. They say we will go out of here the quickest way. As far as I'm concerned the quickest way is not quick enough but soon we will all be home. This day will live long in our hearts. Many was the time when I thought I would not see home again. But here I am and as good as home once again. All I care to do now is go home and the hell with Germany. They have everything coming to them that has come in the past and what's to come in the future. We are sitting now on top of the world. Yippee!!! Once again we live like men and eat like men. The twenty-sixth of April will live inside me for a long time. Thanks to God I will see home once again.

JOHN C. BITZER

LIBERATION DAY
APRIL 26, 1945

I wish I could impress on those that read this the feeling that is in our hearts and minds. Today is Liberation Day and I will never forget it. The K Rations tonight was a dream fulfilled after eating what we have since we have been on this march. Hancock, Miller, McClure and myself saw this day together. I've known these boys since they have been POWs. Miller came to Stalag Luft VI with me and seventy-eight others. It's all been pretty rough but we saw it through although we had our doubts at times. It's good to see two thousand men running around with a good meal in our bellies and happy as larks. Yes, I can't think of much more because my mind is not in shape to do any writing. So I'll close once again.

APRIL 27, 1945

I didn't sleep a wink last night but I just don't particularly care. I am still in Bitterfeld waiting to move out, which should be this morning. We went out into the town and raided a bakery. There were seven of us and the owner, who was a little on the scared side, wanted to give us old bread. We want[ed] fresh bread, so we got the fresh bread and walked out. We didn't give anything for the bread because we wanted to get back at the Jerries for the treatment and the rations we got while on the march. The M.P.s told us, anything we want, to just go and take it. Cameras and field glasses were supposed to have been turned in, so any we found on the civilians we took away from them. At eleven o'clock the trucks came and we took off. It really was good to ride in a good old G.I. truck. We came from Bitterfeld to Halle in forty-five minutes. Here we got set up for a few days to get deloused and get clean clothes and then homeward bound. It's still hard to believe that you're a free man once again after a year and a half of running around in Germany. Today was a full up day and everything that happened pointed to going home once again.

APRIL 28, 1945

The second day of liberation and it's still all a dream. Got my first good night's sleep in three days and I felt like a million. Hoping to get on our way soon. We got registered this morning, name, rank, A.S.N. [serial number], P.O.W. , where and when shot down, etc. We went up and ate chow and, boy, it's sure different from what we have been eating from the Jerries. It just does not seem possible, all of this, after living the life we have for so long a time. It will be hard for a person back home to realize what we have been through. After chow we went up to a house where there was a nice coal burning stove and made us some coffee. Later on, we went to the buildings where the Jerries used to be and raided their clothing store. I got a pair of pants, which I needed bad, and some under-wear and a sweater. There sure is a lot of stuff like clothing and army equipment left here. This used to be a good sized air base until we came along. There are a lot of planes on the field, burnt and full of holes. We sure knocked hell out of this place. The way things look the Jerries sure left in one big hurry. This is an awful big place right by Halle. There is millions of dollars worth of equipment here. If I could only have a G.I. truck, I'd haul a bunch of this stuff home and it would be worth money. Well, another day closer to home. Good night!!!

APRIL 29, 1945

This is another day and it was pretty full. We got up at six today, we are in the army again now. Ate breakfast and came back and cleared up the room. We mosied around all morning, then ate dinner. After dinner, Rub, Handy and myself went walking and saw a lot of stuff left by the Jerries. Tools and machinery galore. We walked and talked with some Jigs. They told us how they advanced from the Rhine to here, it sure must have been a picnic. We got a look at a map and it had the lines Russian and American on it. We sure were lucky to get where we are today. General Hodges 1st Army will remain in my memory for a long time. He sure pushed through to get to us and we had luck with us. Luck was sure against us for a long time but as all things have to change if you stick it out, so did our luck. By the end of May we all hope to be close to home if not home—home sweet home—I never realized how good I had it at home, but by God I'll make up for what I missed.

Poetry

John Bitzer's log included seven poems, most of which were more narratives about the experiences of the prisoners of war than fantasies or longing. A couple of poems were his own, but he also carefully copied poetry that he found scribbled on scraps of paper, written by his comrades in the barracks. Other anonymous poems were widely circulated through stalags all over Nazi-held Europe, sometimes edited and rewritten to put an individual POWs' own imprint on it. Through verse, the men compiled and recorded part of the history they lived through. In "Airman's Lament," a strangely surreal poem, the anonymous poet merged the body of a dying airman with the equipment from his plane's wreckage as the soldier asks his comrades to rebuild the bomber with the parts embedded in his body. (The "con-rod" mentioned in the poem is a connecting rod and the "tappet" is a cylindrical projection that causes motion in the engine.) This poem has another version, titled "A Handsome Young Airman," with a refrain in which the dying airman begs his mother's forgiveness: "I never should have joined the Air Corps, Mother, dear Mother, knew best." In Bitzer's version, the speaker expresses no such regret.

"That Fatal Ride" tells yet another wartime story, commemorating the bravery of the POWs from Stalag Luft VI who endured the torture of being transported across the Baltic Sea, with thousands of men piled into

the suffocating darkness of the ship's hold without food, water, or sanitary conditions for three days. As Bitzer noted, the so-called "Baltic Cruise" in July of 1944 was later deemed a war crime. This poet conveys the horror of the ordeal while raising the question of whether the courage of his comrades would be remembered on the home front.

That Fatal Ride

Tis a most unpleasant story I am about to tell
About the fatal boat ride we all remember so well
That day we loaded up, folks, words cannot express
The agonies we suffered you can hardly guess
Although we're not complaining we took it like real men
But will you folks remember when we're home again.

When they stowed us in that boat hole we thought our time had come
But not a sound was uttered; everything was mum
That sea of stricken faces that you saw down below
You cannot express our feeling but you won't forget, I know
Although we're not complaining, we took it like real men
But will you folks remember when we're home again.

When we climbed below that water line
Jerry riding on top where everything was fine
A prayer was on our lips, I know no hypocrites were there
The sweat rolled off our bodies most were stripped down bare
Although we're not complaining we took it like real men
But will you folks remember when we're home again.

Your husband, son, or sweetheart, may be in there
But did he complain, no Sir! His thoughts were with you

Oh! If I can spare this torture I won't say a word
Everyone must have thought the same though not a word occurred.

A little ray of sunshine, skies of velvet blue
But take them all away, folks, and their value is high
That's what happened on that boat and we were prepared to die.
Although we're not complaining we took it like real men
But will you folks remember when we're home again.

For forty-eight hours of hell on earth we rode that stormy sea
Ten men were crowded in a place where one should be
Although we're not complaining we took it like real men
But will you folks remember when we're home again.

One kriegie weaker than the rest who couldn't stand no more
Jumped overboard that night and tried to swim ashore
But wait a minute what was that! Then all hell tore loose
A watery grave in the Baltic was that poor guy's noose
So when you start complaining and pleasures seem so few
Think of Stalag VI and what we all went through.

Airman's Lament

A poor aviator lay dying
At the end of a bright summer's day
His comrades were gathered round him
To carry the fragments away

The engine was piled on his wishbone
The sparkplugs stuck out of his head
From the small of his back came the con-rod
It was plain he would shortly be dead.

He spat out a valve and a gasket
And stirred in the sump where he lay
And then to his wandering comrades
These brave words he did say

> Take the tappets out of my larynx
> Take the spark plugs out of my brain
> From the small of my back take the con-rod
> And assemble the engine again.

I'll be riding the clouds in the morning
With no rotary before to cuss
Shake the lead from your feet and get busy
There's another lad needing this bus.

> Who minds to the dust returning
> Who shrinks from the sable shore
> Where the light and haughty yearning
> of the soul shall be no more.

So stand with your glasses steady
Here's health to those that fly
Here's a toast to the dead already
And here's to the next man that dies.

A Gunner's Day

A gunner's day is never done
Up at dawn before the sun
With the roar of engines in his head
Wishing he could have stayed in bed.

Chow at four, fried eggs and such
Won't have time to eat very much
Briefing at five the crew is all here
Everyone anxious to be up in the air

See to your chute, ammunition and gun
For the boys all know it's not all for fun
Jerry will be up there high in the blue
Waiting for someone perhaps for you.

Take-off at six or maybe six thirty
Hope no one has a gun that's dirty
Form with the group at 12,000 feet
See that formation! They're neat

Put on your mask the air is getting thin
Off to battle some with a grin
We're over the channel now test your guns
Enemy coast here comes the fun

Flak at six flak at twelve
Look out boys, they're giving us hell
Here's the fighters coming in low
Maybe they're ours; don't shoot till you know

Our escort is here they're never late
They're fighting fools
each man and his ship
There isn't a Jerry they couldn't whip

The air is cold just fifty below
Turn up the heat or you'll freeze a toe
A sharp look out boys, the target's near
We don't care to meet the enemy here

Here's the target plenty of flak
Bombs away Boys, we turn back
Coming out of the sun there! Enemy ships
Aim true boys we've still got more trips

> There goes one down another one too
> Our fighters see none get through,
> There's flames in the sky another goes down
> The pilot bails out makes it to the ground

Then in our tail the guns start to roar
There's blood on your guns you shoot as before
Your ship is hit but still flies through the air
You think of loved ones or whisper a prayer

> Smoke from the target leaps high in the sky
> We'll show those Jerries we know how to fly
> The fighters have left they know what's best
> Our fighters got some we got the rest

We've been up six hours two hours to go
Though we're doing two hundred it seems pretty slow
England at last the tail gunners learn
We think of buddies who will not return

> We're over the field the crew gives a sigh
> We've finished another to do or to die
> Wheels touch the ground with a screech and bump
> Our ship brought us back over the hump

We're tired and dirty, thirsty and sore
The sun has gone down an hour before
First clean your gun and do it good, boys,
For that gun is life: his, mine, or yours.

Burst of Flak

You're flying in the sky so blue
The flak it comes so straight and true
It hits the plane it drives you back
And the cause of it all was a burst of flak

> The fighters then with a bloody thirst
> To give you a taste of twenty mm bursts
> It knows your buddies on their backs
> And the cause of it all a burst of flak

You grab your chute, head for the door
Cause your plane is disabled you're wounded and sore
As you hit the silk the sky goes black
And the cause of it all: a burst of flak

> You flop through the air all is quiet
> The ship goes down that good old kite
> Then you hit the ground with a smack
> The cause of it all, a burst of flak

The farmers and soldiers come over the hill
With blood in their eyes ready to kill
They lift you up and give you a crack
The cause of it all, a burst of flak

> They get your crew, march you through town
> So people can watch with a grin and frown
> They put you in jail a filthy old shack
> The cause of it all a burst of flak.

Then you go to a P.O.W. camp
Where your friend is the Red Cross stamp

You sleep on the floor it hurts your back
The cause of it all a burst of Flak

> We sit and think of our girls so true
> And the boys still flying in the blue,
> Of pillows and sheets that made your sack,
> The cause of it all, a burst of Flak.

Christmas as a P.O.W.

Today is another. My third one from home
With no place to go but this lager to roam
I'll try and I'll try to treat it with regard
Although it may be a little bit hard.

Today is another it hardly seems so
I'm thinking of loved ones I saw long ago
The loved ones I saw yes, day in and day out
I'll see them again some day without a doubt.

Today is another I hope and I pray
That I'll be out and away from this some day
Then this day will mean something sincere
And I'll be with you again dear
Oh ever so near.

S/SGT. JOHN C. BITZER
DECEMBER 25, 1944
STALAG LUFT IV

Your Weekly Letter

A thought of love, a word of cheer
Your weekly message to someone dear
A line of words from your heart comes stealing
To let her know just how you are feeling.

You write about weather and say that you're well
But there's so many things that you cannot tell
You talk about old times and how much you miss her
And hope to come back once more to kiss her.

She doesn't know what you're going through
It would be mighty hard if she only knew
The long hard days just sitting here
Alone with your thoughts and your heart full of fear

That you never return to your home again
All hope is gone . . . you live in vain.
Yet as each week comes you rewrite once more
The same old lines as the week before

And pray when she receives them she'll never know better
What you couldn't write in your weekly letter.

JANUARY 28, 1945

My Buddies

HONOR ROLL
Lt. J.Y Schrero
Lt. J. Lamarski
Lt. L. Doan
S/Sgt. D.L. Troxell
Lt. M. Kent
T/Sgt. H.B. May
S/Sgt. H.L. Miller
S/Sgt. H. Holland
S/Sgt. J.C. Bitzer
S/Sgt. W. Dickerman

They said they died in glory
Whatever that may be
If dying in a burst of flame is glory
Then that's not for me.

In the briefing room that morning
They sat with clear eyes and strong hearts
Just a few of the many gunners
Determined to do their parts.

My buddies had the guts all right
They sought not glory nor fame
They knew they had a job to do
And other crews felt the same.

But death had the final word
For in its log it wrote their names
And my buddies died that morning
In glory and a burst of flame.

3

PART THREE

BILL BLACKMON'S STORY

Bill Blackmon was eighteen years old when he enlisted in the Army Air Corps. "I thought I was immune to it, to being killed. I didn't think they could hurt me," Blackmon said about his youthful naïveté. Within the year, he would be captured by the Nazis. Above, Blackmon prior to shipping out to Europe in 1943; below, he is pictured just after his release from Stalag XVII a year and a half later.

Bill Blackmon

During his stay in Stalag XVII B, Steve Carano's buddy, Bill "Blackie" Blackmon, did not keep a journal and does not recall ever seeing Carano's Wartime Log. He was not aware of when the YMCA distributed them. Yet with the recollection and storytelling ability of a true raconteur, Blackmon kept his own record deep in his memories, ready to be called up in intricate detail. During my interviews with him in 2005 in Baton Rouge, Louisiana, he talked about his experiences in Stalag XVII B, and the stories began to weave together with his Louisiana childhood, spent in a Methodist orphanage, providing a rich oral history that calls forth something mysterious and wonderful about the human psyche. In those memories lie a young man's unquestioning faith in his own survival, and, despite the harshest of treatment, his ability to exercise compassion, if not forgiveness, about the two incarcerations he endured in the first twenty years of his life. In our many subsequent telephone conversations, he compared his boyhood years in the orphanage—witnessing brutality, harsh work and beatings—to life as young prisoner of war in Stalag XVII. Both experiences involved psychological resourcefulness and a strong will to survive. Bill Blackmon's memories bring to mind how, as William Faulkner wrote in his famous Nobel Prize speech, the human spirit might not only "endure, but prevail."

THE ORPHANAGE, 1932–36

In 1932, one of the worst years of the Depression, Kate Blackmon was a young Louisiana mother with three children and no way to feed them. Her husband had been an adequate provider until hard times came, but then, feeling helpless to support his young children on desolate farmland in southern Louisiana, he moved his family to Monroe and abandoned them there. Out in the country where they had lived near a tiny town called Maugham, there was not even transportation to school for six-year-old Bill, so the move to Monroe allowed him to start first grade, and brought his mother closer to her own family in the city. "We were starving," Bill Blackmon explained, shrugging away the memory at age eighty-two. But in those difficult Depression years, Kate couldn't find enough food for the table even in Monroe, and in two more years, there was yet another move in store for him, as his mother faced a terrible decision: a few miles away in Ruston, the Methodist orphanage offered a warm shelter with nutritious food for her children.

She left her two sons and small daughter there, little suspecting the kind of Dickensian nightmare her children would enter. Eight-year-old Bill, heartbroken at the sight of the car disappearing down the road with his mother and uncle, stared disbelievingly at the trail of thick dust stirred by the tires. Even decades later, he could not forget the sight of those smoke-like plumes and the hopelessness that swept over him on that terrible day. Frightened by the strange environment in the home, Bill, the eldest of the three, cried himself to sleep that first night, though he was the kind of boy who was too proud to let anyone see.

Beatings were frequent at the orphanage and public shaming was a routine form of punishment. The punishment for bed-wetting was an icy cold bath, administered by the matron's husband, a man named Manning. After that, the child would be made to stand, shivering and ashamed, at the foot of the stairs leading up to the other boys' rooms, wrapped in his bedsheet with the damp section over his nose, forcing him to inhale the acrid odor of his urine. That way, said Blackmon, the offending child was on public display for any bully to ridicule. All day the child wore a diaper cruelly pinned into place beneath his coveralls by the matron's husband. Bill took courage in telling himself that his mother would come back soon to get him and his younger brother and sister. His sister, Katie, small and pretty, became the pet of the older girls who would stroke her hair and let her sit on their laps while he and his brother had to fend off the fists and taunts of bullies. They envied the good treatment their sister received.

On visitor's day one Sunday afternoon, his mother entered the orphanage with a strange man, a new husband who had reluctantly told his bride that he could afford to support only one of her children. She had returned to the orphanage to make that difficult choice. Though Bill had often lifted his shirt to show his mother the marks left on his back from the routine beatings, somehow she assured herself that her two sons could survive the place. Besides, what else did she have to offer them, besides the promise that she would get them as soon as their new step-father could provide for them? She found Katie and told her daughter to pack up her few belongings. Unable to bear telling her two sons of her choice, she took Katie without even seeing the boys.

Bill had always thought that, as the oldest boy, he was his mother's favorite, and it was incredible to him that now she had chosen his younger sister. Devastated at being abandoned yet again, he plotted to run away at the first chance. Two years, after breakfast, he slipped out to the side yard of the orphanage and then headed down the road that wound through sparse piney woods, his bare feet making tracks in the same dirt that had settled behind his mother's car as she left for Monroe with little Katie so long ago.

But it was hard for a ten-year-old boy to escape notice, especially if his face was frightened and he clutched his only belongings in his thin arms. Even so, Bill had walked fifteen miles down the road when a car roared behind him. It was an official from the orphanage, a man who swept him up by the seat of his pants and deposited him in the back seat of the automobile. Bill hadn't even been able to see the man's face, so quickly had he yanked him up. It was the first time he'd ridden in a car since he'd made the long drive to the orphanage, when his mother had been at the wheel, and now he had the same destination.

Standing in front of the boys' cottage where he'd been assigned to live, Bill was amazed that the superintendent, Brother Vaughn, who was known to be strict, merely lectured him and made him promise never to run away again. When Bill turned to leave, though, the force of a kick nearly drove him against a wall. Brother Vaughn aimed his shoe directly between the boy's legs, knowing how to target his small charges. "When

I was in that orphanage, I had some bad times," Blackmon remembered, shaking his head at the understatement.

Every weekend, attendance at prayer services was required and on Sundays the children marched to the nearby church in Ruston, clutching envelopes with their names scrawled on them. Inside was a penny, and an empty envelope—signifying a lost or stolen penny—would mean a beating. From the time he was eight until he was thirteen, Bill listened to full sermons every Sunday, fearful of beatings if his attention flagged or his penny was lost. After school or on weekends, the children worked in the alfalfa or pea fields, helping to support the orphanage. If one of them playfully tossed a clod of dirt or took too long to rest, the farm manager's assistants promised them a beating that night. "That was the hardest part," Blackmon remembered, "waiting three or four hours for a beating that you knew would come. Why didn't he just give it to me then?"

Most of the assistants had grown up in the orphanage and, knowing no other world, stayed on as adults. One assistant, "Peg" Baker, had a homemade wooden leg fashioned from a thick stick used to support tomato vines. Their own boyhoods at the orphanage had taught them that harsh punishment, not compassion, was the proper treatment for children, and they guarded their young charges as carefully as they had been looked after.

Several years passed before Bill attempted another escape. One night, after the lights were out in the boys' hallway, he had heard a commotion on the floor below that woke him and his buddies. Hearing horrific screams, the children rushed to the railing of the stairs and witnessed, from the safe darkness of the landing, the matron beating a teenaged boy in the head with the spike of her high-heeled shoe. Her husband, the same man who had twice humiliated Bill for bed-wetting, held the boy's feet as he lay thrashing on the floor. His "crime" was peeking in the window while she and her husband had sex. The boy, Ollie Taylor, died a few months later. Bill was never certain of the cause of death. But he was certain of one thing: he had to leave the orphanage. This time, he was older, thirteen, and he knew exactly where to run. He hitchhiked thirty-two miles to his uncle's home in Monroe, where his uncle ran a honky-tonk called The Blue Heaven Night Club. On the way, Bill camped for the night on a riverbank, shivering in the cold and hiding from a nearby houseboat moored on the bank. When he made it to Monroe, at last, someone was willing to save him. Drinking ice-cold Dr Peppers in The Blue Heaven, peeping at the dancers, and riding the bicycle his uncle bought him, Bill had found a home. For the next several months, the family tried to talk him into returning to the orphanage because his brother was still there, but Bill insisted on his freedom, and it wasn't long before his family retrieved his brother. Determined never to be imprisoned again, he worked and studied hard in the lean times of the late 1930s, while, in what seemed like another world, Hitler's Third Reich was surging to power in Europe.

THE ARMY, 1942–1944

When the war broke out, Blackmon enlisted in the Army Air Force as soon as he was old enough, certain that he would otherwise soon be drafted. Eager to explore the world beyond Louisiana, he wanted choices about where he went and how he served. But when he weighed in, the scales registered only 112 pounds—underweight by any standard, especially on his six-foot frame. For days before going down to the Army enlistment station on November 23, 1942, he ate as many bananas as he could stand, and his quick-gain strategy worked. The Army found him acceptable at 116 pounds and sent him to the reception center in Beauregard for aptitude testing. Later, he was shipped him off to Aircraft Mechanics School in Amarillo, then to gunnery school in Las Vegas, and finally on to Texas, to complete his preparation as a flier with the Army Air Force, which was where he met Steve Carano.

A fresh-faced boy of eighteen, Blackmon enjoyed the camaraderie he found with his new crewmates. In the Army mess hall, he ate fairly decently, and his buddies were good company. Later, in England, one of his friends, Tom O'Brien, remembered Blackmon as the "kind of young soldier who would often get up early to go to breakfast with me, even on days that his own crew wasn't scheduled to fly a mission."

Flying on the B-17s out of Ridgewell, Blackmon, like so many other young men, thought the war was a grand adventure. In phase training in the Texas desert, he'd strafed cacti and buzzed the pilot's house while his relatives waved from below. To an eighteen-year-old kid, the European war didn't yet seem terribly different from training. By day, the fighters roared through the blue skies over France, Holland, and Germany, dodging Germany's best fighter, the Focke-Wulf 190. Assigned to the tail gunner position, Blackmon aimed his sites at the painted red grins leering from the noses of enemy aircraft and even managed to shoot down one of the elusive 190s. Though the plane on which his friend Steve Carano was serving as a replacement radio operator had gone down, young Blackmon never thought it could happen to him.

At night a German fighter routinely flew over the Ridgewell aerodome, the sound of its engines recognizable as enemy aircraft. It was regular, always around ten o'clock. "Bedcheck Charlie, we called him," laughed Blackmon, and even then the danger did not seem real.

It was a boy's game for Blackmon during those first twelve or thirteen missions—"you flew that many," he says, "and you felt lucky"—until one day in November, when flak ripped into his plane, forcing two of his crewmates, the bombardier and the navigator, to bail out. When the plane crash-landed in England, the interior of the nose, where the two men had been, was covered with their blood. These were the first losses Blackmon had witnessed, and the danger suddenly struck him hard. During a break given the crew at Southport Rest Home, on England's west coast, he took long walks on the windy beach, remembering the blood-smeared plane and his two downed comrades. He shook off the boyish adventurism.

"I was just a teenager but I realized then that flak is not just smoke going by, jarring the plane when it was close," he said. "They got a darn projectile that's about a foot long and they're shooting it at your plane! I loved it at first and didn't think a thing of that flak. I guess I thought I was immune to it, to being killed. I didn't think they could hurt me. But after I went to that rest home, I had second thoughts, I had time to think about it."

Sobered by the realization of his own mortality, Blackmon made it through seventeen missions—an unusual record. "Every time I'd see flak, they'd always shoot and burst before, but they'd be closer each time. If the next one was coming toward me, then I'd look for the next one, and I'd think, my god, they're going to hit us." Twenty-five missions was a man's ticket out of the war, but few made it that long.

As Germans captured more and more American fliers, the Army brought in a soldier named Lee C. Gordon, who had escaped from Stalag XVII B, to offer "escape and evasion" tactics to the men in case of capture. He was a short, slight man, and his modest appearance belied the derring-do behind his escape. Three or four times, he had eluded the guards at Stalag XVII only to be recaptured, but, a master of escape, he was never deterred. On his final effort, Gordon had dug a tunnel beneath his barrack and finally crawled his way to freedom in the Alps. He explained the system by which the Germans punished would-be escapists: if caught, they would go to the brig, heated with a small radiator. In the middle of an Austrian winter, Gordon said, the heated brig was actually better than a bunk in a drafty barrack.

Though Blackmon enjoyed hearing Gordon's stories, capture was far from his mind. It couldn't happen to him, he thought. He was too close to the twenty-fifth mission that would bring him home.

By March 6, 1944, the day the Berlin blitz began, Blackmon had become an experienced flyer. In the biggest flying mission of the European war, his B-17 was one of thousands flying in an awesome formation over Berlin, terrifying the Germans as they poured relentlessly over the city in wave after wave. From the ground, it appeared as if the planes would never stop coming. Berliners remaining in the city, holed up in ruins, could watch the sky for a full half-hour before a single onslaught of bombers ended. Each stream was over ninety miles long, a mile wide, and half a mile deep. During those famous deadly raids, 701 American airmen were lost, along with sixty-nine planes, but greater damage by far was inflicted upon Berlin. As he watched men bail out of flaming bombers into enemy territory, Blackmon told himself that he'd rather be killed than captured in combat.

On a cool day in late April, Blackmon suited up for his seventeenth mission out of the Ridgewell base. He was now well past the "hump," and on his way to the charmed twenty-fifth mission. He'd celebrated his twentieth birthday eight days before, but it felt as if the last few months had aged him far more than a year. Though one never got used to the danger, Blackmon knew he did his job well. He'd shot down a Focke-Wulf 190, one of Germany's best fighters, and an ME 109. The assignment on the morning of April 28, 1944, seemed relatively easy, especially after the harrowing raids over Berlin only weeks before. There were no "milk runs" any more, but this time they were flying lead plane in a bombing mission over France, a fairly short distance.

Flak struck once, twice, three times, but still the plane remained stable. In the waist, behind the pilot and copilot, Blackmon and his crew members searched the skies for enemy aircraft but never saw the Nazi fighter. Then a direct hit rocked the bomber and sent it spiraling, pieces flying into the air. "Thank god we dropped those bombs before we were hit," Blackmon said. In the chaos, Blackmon saw the radio operator, J. W. Padgett, release the red handle on the waist door and jump from the plane, his parachute strapped to his back.

As the plane went into an abrupt dive, the impact threw the other waist gunner against the tail wheel strut, and the force of the rapid descent sent the weight of Blackmon's body against his. "I can remember him screaming in my ear and I could feel his head crushing underneath my weight in that plane, in that dive."

From the pilot came a barely heard order to bail. Blackmon struggled to reach his parachute, which had been thrown around the plane. "I liked to jerk my neck off trying to get my parachute. I reached out and got a corner of the door and just pulled myself out, with one side of the chute connected and falling. I remember all the parachutists who would tell us how to jump, to put your head down and roll out and don't pull your rip-cord. Well, I didn't because I was trying to get the chute hooked on the other side. Then I remembered they said, 'look straight out if you want to determine what altitude you are.' So I did that, and I slowed my descent more. I knew when to pull that chute." The advice he'd heard in flight school ran through his mind, like landing on the balls of his feet with his knees bent. Upon landing, he was supposed to jump up and get the air out of his parachute, lest he be dragged across the terrain. Blackmon made it, but above him the plane broke up into fiery pieces. Of the nine men aboard, only three escaped alive, landing on the runway of the airfield they had just bombed.

Years later, at a POW reunion arranged by the National Ex-Prisoners of War Organization, Blackmon met a veteran who had been the copilot on a bomber that had accompanied his in formation on his last flight. The man shook his head, still remembering the sight of Blackmon's plane disintegrating in the sky. "I saw your plane blow up," he told Blackmon. "I followed it to the ground. It broke up into pieces. I didn't see a soul get out. You know, that was my first mission and I came goddamn near to quitting right then when I saw that. I just knew it killed every one of you."

Yet some had managed to survive. On the ground, Blackmon struggled to free himself from the chute and get his bearings, blood streaming from a wound to his head. He and J. W. Padgett were quickly surrounded by German soldiers, who loaded them into a weapons carrier with seats on both sides. They rolled over the rough ground, bouncing in the rear of the carrier.

In the train station in Orleans, a French gendarme wearing an oversized coat that looked warm and even "dressy" to Blackmon, eyed the two new prisoners of war warily. Then he thrust two fingers in the air, briefly making a victory sign and winked at Blackmon before turning away. The quick gesture of sympathy was enough to inspire the young Blackmon with heroic ideas of escape. Hoping to find Resistance fighters among the French, he whispered to Padgett that he was going to flee. But with a wife and children at home in the States, Padgett felt he couldn't take the risk and urged Blackmon to stay with him.

"Padgett was entirely the opposite of Steve Carano; he was a nervous wreck. How could I leave him?" asked Blackmon, decades later. So on they went, constantly under guard by the Germans, to recuperate from their wounds in a Paris hospital.

From his room on the eighth floor of the hospital, Blackmon looked down and watched Parisians and Germans walking along the Champs Elysee as if nothing were wrong with the world. "There were people on the sidewalks drinking wine at tables—this was in April—and here I am, a prisoner, right in downtown Paris. We'd see these pretty women with German soldiers. There was a German soldier, walking with his girlfriend, but he looks up and he sees me looking out the window and I'm trying to soak in all the view and he pulls his gun out and aims it at me as if to say, 'you better get back in there or I'll shoot you.' Of course, I pop my head back in. He looked like an officer." Shaken from his envious reverie, Blackmon drew back quickly from the window. Who knew what could happen in the enemies' world?

After he recovered, the Germans shipped him on a boxcar to Frankfurt to be processed. Blackmon, stepping off the train near Dulag Luft with other new prisoners of war, found a crowd of angry German women and old men at the station, swarming around the Americans, beating them with their only weapons—black umbrellas or wooden canes. To the German civilians, the drone of the American B-17s and B-24s was terrifying, signaling the devastation of their cities and consequent loss of life. The young men who flew the bombers were, to them, "terrorfliegers," not the often-frightened young men who were carrying out the missions.

"We'd just about flattened their whole city," said Blackmon, remembering the shattered train station at Frankfurt. Fearful of even greater retribution, the Americans silently fended off the blows from German umbrellas as best they could, and when one soldier lost his temper, cursing at the women, the others hissed, "Shut your goddamn mouth, you'll get us all in trouble!" German guards shuttled them past the angry townspeople and down into the basement of the station where they would be safe.

At Dulag Luft, the interrogation center for newly captured soldiers, Blackmon remained in a small cell in solitary confinement for three days, with a diet of hard black bread and water. The German interrogator, in perfect English, repeatedly asked for more information than name, rank and serial number, and each time Blackmon refused to answer. When the interrogator left, Blackmon squirmed in discomfort on the hard bench, twisting to find a more agreeable way to sit for those long hours. Painted on the wooden slat behind him, he saw the comic face of "Kilroy," his long cartoon nose and big eyes peeping over the back of the bench. Everywhere, it seemed, GIs scribbled the silly face with the inscription "Kilroy was here," and the cartoon had quickly become a legend in American popular culture.

Even in the German interrogation center some previous American soldier had scrawled "Kilroy was here" beneath the cartoon and it was enough to let Blackmon know that he was not alone. For the first time since his capture, he laughed, a reaction that would help him keep his equilibrium in the many months to come. Others had been there before and others would come later, and somehow he, too, would get through. The legendary "Kilroy" had destroyed the sense of isolation that the Germans hoped would cause their captives to "crack" and give valuable information for either their intelligence or propaganda machines. There was something mysterious and comforting about the ubiquity of "Kilroy" wherever a GI went. If you didn't see Kilroy in a place, reports Bill Davidge, "then you drew him there." So pervasive were the poems and cartoons that, years later, Blackmon remembered a poem in which yet another anonymous GI gave a twist on the joke:

> I danced with glee
> I jumped with joy
> Because I was here before Kilroy.
> I hate to spoil your little joke
> But I was here and my pencil broke.

STALAG XVII, 1944–1945

When Blackmon finally arrived at Stalag XVII, there was Steve Carano, clapping him on the back, still the "big brother" he had been in Texas when they had flown together and, later, in England. It seemed like many months since they'd seen each other, though only five had passed. Though he'd lost weight and his face was gaunt, Carano still had his rakish grin. During the months that followed, Blackmon often visited his old buddy, a few barracks over, for a chat about the war and a cup of the strong coffee Carano always seemed to have. With a makeshift radio in his bunk, Carano often had news of the war, and it gave the younger man hope.

It wasn't long before Blackmon encountered another familiar name: Lee C. Gordon. But this man with curly, chin-length black hair, a thin moustache, and an Australian accent was not at all like the escape artist that Blackmon had met in England. Soon, Blackmon learned the mystery behind the two Lee C. Gordons. To throw off the Germans, a prisoner exchange had been arranged for another man to take the original Gordon's place during head-count. "Kurt" Kurtenbach, the sergeant who had been elected camp leader of Stalag XVII—the "Man of Confidence" in charge of POW negotiations with the camp administrators—was a master at negotiating among the prisoners as well as with the guards. He arranged for an Australian prisoner of war, housed in a nearby camp to be smuggled into Stalag XVII as the new "Lee C. Gordon." With an imposter in place, Gordon had known that the Germans wouldn't search for him or punish his bunkmates for his absence. For his Australian stand-in, the treatment from the Germans would be better on the American side. In the Christmas program, the new Lee C. Gordon played the "ballet dancer deluxe," and he would occasionally test recently arrived POWs by gently patting their legs and sliding his hand up until he was discouraged. "I let him know I wasn't interested," Blackmon said. "But I don't know what happened, you know, when the lights went out. What other people did wasn't my business."

During the year he spent in Stalag XVII, Blackmon witnessed five or six suicides: men who deliberately ran into the guard wire so that the German guards would shoot them. "They just couldn't handle it anymore," he says. "It was awful, I tell you that. We'd freeze to death, standing stark naked getting deloused. Little things would rile you up in prison. Somebody'd take a little bit more than you thought was their fair share of a Red Cross parcel." Even if it was only the "klim" milk, a pow-ered substance with a taste far from actual milk, the goods were precious luxuries.

From barrack 29-A, next to the fence separating the Americans from the Russian POWs, Blackmon could look out his window and, every so often, see dead men, starved Russians, lying out in the open. To the Nazis, the Russian Slavs were "sub-human," and the horrible abuses that Blackmon witnessed on the other side of the wire were systematically being carried out against millions of Russians across the continent. Somehow, one of the Russians managed to smuggle himself into the American camp. With his toes lost to severe frostbite from the cold and exposure on the Russian side, he walked with a hobble. Yet his eyes flashed beneath his shock of black hair and bushy eyebrows, and the man had a fierce, deter-mined bearing that won him the admiration and respect of the American POWs. "Despite all that he went through to survive," Blackmon said, "the Russian Army probably killed him when they found him." (As Alexander Solzhenitsyn pointed out in *The Gulag Archipelago,* it was a tragic irony that the Russian Army sent their own men, under suspicion of treason, to death camps after "liberating" them from the Germans.)

With six of his barrack comrades, Blackmon began to dig a tunnel out of the camp, slowly inching through the earth beneath a lower bunk with only a coffee can as a shovel. Beyond the wire fence, the Alps looked like friendly territory, a path to freedom in nearby Switzerland. Blackmon remembered Lee C. Gordon's stories of escape from Stalag XVII and in the winter, the thought of the brig with its radiator didn't seem quite as bad as the bitter cold in the barrack. The first time the Germans caught a prisoner escaping, they sentenced him to seven days in the brig with only bread and water. If caught a second time, seven days were added to his sen-tence, and so on, until on the fourth time the Germans would start over again, not able to accommodate a single prisoner for so many weeks in the solitary confinement of the brig. If a prisoner was caught beyond the fence, though, the punishment was instant death by shooting.

When Blackmon confided his escape plans to Carano, he didn't find the encouragement he had expected. "We'll get loose soon," Carano told him, still playing the big brother to his younger friend. "I don't want you doing that, digging a tunnel." Carano's suggestion to wait it out seemed like a kind of giving up, and still Blackmon and his comrades dug, feeling at least a little power in the act of tunneling. It gave them a goal when they woke up in the mornings, and it gave them hope when they went to bed at night.

For three months, Blackmon and his friends scraped away down in the tunnel, removing the dirt by filling their pockets and then secretively shaking it out as they walked in the compound. It was hard, painstaking work that was all too quickly undone by a guard they nicknamed "the mole." Carrying a steel stick with a handle, "the mole" routinely shoved the tip into the ground, searching for the hollows that would indicate a tunnel. He'd uncovered enough escape attempts that his German superiors had given him a medal, and Blackmon's subterranean efforts fell prey to the probings of the steel stick. Once caught, he and his comrades were forced to fill in the tunnel, and to find another source of hope.

Blackmon said as a POW you "never lost faith that you'd get out—you knew the Allies were winning, but survival through the brutal cold and malnutrition were the issue." Somehow, they found humor wherever they could, and it was humor as well as faith that kept them going. One cold night, when the lights went out in barrack 29-A, the men were trying to sleep when one soldier loudly broke wind. There was a slight pause, then, from the other side of the barrack came a voice, "Speak again, sweet lips, I'll find you." The entire barrack erupted in laughter. The sudden outbursts of hilarity must have unsettled the German guards, confused by these men who found humor in such strange ways. "When you've been there, anything that's humorous at all, you're going to laugh," Blackmon said. "You've been penned up for more than a year, and it's hell. And anything's funny to you." It was one way, at least, of surviving.

The crystal radio sets the men were able to devise had also begun to give them hope. In their bunks, they huddled around the primitive sets, struggling to make sense of the words that emerged through the crackling reception. The Battle of the Bulge was going well for Germany, they heard, and in dismay some of the POWs ruefully changed their slogan to "Out the Gate in '48," assuming that it would take a few more years for the Allies to win. Later, the reports gave them reason to cheer. Surely it would be over soon.

Toward the end, when the war seemed to be winding down, the temper of the guards rose. "They were really brutal toward the last," reported Blackmon. "We'd bombed their wives and kids. The Americans bombed a railroad station at Krems and killed civilians, the families of guards. They'd come up to your bunk and blow their whistle right in your ear and if you didn't jump right out of bed, they'd start kicking you. I got kicked in the butt four or five times when I was in there. But after that orphanage, Stalag XVII didn't seem so bad."

Despite the brutality, the cold, and the meager provisions, Blackmon never doubted he was going to live. "I just knew I was going to get through it. I just knew it," he said.

LIBERATION, APRIL–MAY 1945

Along with his fellow prisoners from Stalag XVII B, Blackmon began the eighteen-day march to freedom on the cold morning of April 8, 1945. As the bedraggled POWs began their long expedition, at the same time, under Hitler's orders, efforts were also being made to evacuate survivors from the death camps across Germany, Poland, and Austria. The path of one of those evacuations, of prisoners from Mecklenburg, intersected that of the Americans from Stalag XVII. It was the sound the men heard first, a moaning like wind, and then the starving evacuees came stumbling into sight. It was the most unforgettable moment of Blackmon's entire war experience, the first glimpse that the Stalag XVII refugees had of the war's deepest horror. A straggly line of Jewish prisoners, staggering in filthy striped uniforms and caps, came into view, led by Nazi storm troopers who shoved aside the American POWS for this agonized group, marching in the opposite direction. "They were gaunt, hollow-eyed. Like skeletons. They looked awful," Blackmon remembered. The road led directly through the concentration camp, newly abandoned, and Blackmon feared this was where the Germans would leave them. Silence fell over the Americans as they watched, dumbstruck, while storm troopers kicked and struck those emaciated prisoners with the butts of their guns. Barely able to move, the prisoners dragged themselves and each other along. A young boy, unable to walk, sagged between two adults, barely stronger than he, who struggled to carry him. Blood streamed from his bony knees to his ankles as his companions dragged him along on the road. When storm troopers spotted the boy, they yanked him off to the side and summarily shot him through the head. "Point-blank," said Blackmon. "His cap flew off his head, about five feet from his body. He was only about eight or nine years old." The others wearily continued on their impossible march to doom. Down the path, Blackmon saw the bodies of several others from the death camp, shot point-blank, their limbs crumpled jaggedly on the ground. It was the caps that Blackmon could force himself to glance at, not the dead faces—the caps that had flown from their heads with the force of the Nazi bullets. Even decades later, the sight of those killings haunted his dreams.

Unbeknownst to Blackmon, one of his fellow POWs from Stalag XVII, Irving J. Mills, saw the same horrific scene and alluded to it in a journal he kept along the march, which he later typed and titled "Eagles Can Walk":

> Today saw a sight never will forget. There is much truth in our propaganda about the anti-Semitic feeling here. The treatment is unbelievable! This was our first encounter with the Nazi treatment of the Jewish race. We met approximately three hundred of them marching in the opposite direction. Judging from their clothes, they had been, at one time, very prosperous but now they had degenerated into a dirty, starved, and completely beaten mass that was hard to recognize as being human beings. They were literally dropping like flies as they dragged along. Those unfortunate enough to drop received no aid whatsoever from their own group and their filthy, revolting guards would dispatch them from this world with their rifle butts rather than waste a single cartridge. Some of our own guards tried to apologize for this demonstration but from that day on, we hated the Germans as a group.

Yet along the way a young, stronger Jewish prisoner shot the Americans a determined smile and flashed a "thumbs up" with his fist held at his waist, a surreptitious signal of victory to Bill Blackmon and his buddies. "He was a bold man," Blackmon said, reflecting on the memory years later. "If the storm troopers had seen him do that, they'd have killed him. It was a brave thing for him to do, to tell us, 'we'll get 'em.' It was uplifting for all of us. If he could do that, then we all could get through."

As they neared their destination, the American POWs grew bolder, and one of Blackmon's companions, a man named Johnston from Sykeston, Missouri, stopped in the middle of the road to cook an egg given him by a farm woman. He made a small fire with a match he had bummed from a villager and, with a coffee can and water, proceeded to boil the egg, a luxury that he hadn't eaten in well over a year. Johnston was crouching protectively over his mouth-watering delicacy when he saw the tall boots of a storm trooper stop beside him. Blackmon watched, amazed, as his friend ignored the Nazi's order to extinguish the fire. "I'm boiling my egg," Johnston told the storm trooper, never taking his eyes off his precious project. "I'll be through in just a minute."

Outraged, the German kicked the egg to the other side of the road, then brought his boot against Johnston's head, knocking him over. Blackmon was sure his friend would be shot, but the storm trooper moved on. Years later, thinking about that audacious act, he called Johnston. "Do you remember getting kicked in the head by that storm trooper?" he asked.

Johnston well remembered the episode, but it wasn't the kick that lingered in his memory; it was the egg. "I wasn't worried about my head," he told Blackmon." I wanted that egg." The accumulated hunger had nearly overwhelmed their senses.

Once near Braunau they set up makeshift camps to wait for the American Army. When the liberating troops arrived, shocked by the horrors they had witnessed in the Nazi-occupied lands, they rounded up the German guards who had supervised the march to Braunau, and then turned to the newly freed POWs. "You got anything against anybody, you just take him out in the woods with this," they told their fellow Americans, brandishing a pistol. A few former prisoners sought out a particular guard and punched him in the face. Others accepted the offer of a pistol and selected a German guard, personally hated, to march him off into the woods. Gun shots would erupt, then the former prisoner returned alone.

"But I couldn't do that," Blackmon said. "I couldn't kill anybody unless he was shooting at me. Just for calling you a name or blowing a whistle in your ear or knocking you? I wasn't brought up that way." Despite the rough years in the orphanage, he had learned not to kill men who were not trying to kill him. For him, such unnecessary killing lay outside the grim boundaries of war.

An elation set in during the giddy days following liberation, an exhilarating, confusing chaos. At least two memoirs of liberation refer to the less-than-admirable way that some American troops behaved. In *The Flame Keepers,* a memoir of life in Stalag XVII, Ned Handy recounts protecting a German farmwoman from his American liberators, who tended to see people in more black-and-white terms than some of the freed POWs, who had occasionally been able to see the humanity in some of the weary

German guards. Irving J. Mills elliptically refers in his journal to a hidden history of the post-liberation days: "We did not leave the woods [around Braunau] until the sixth of May and during that time the conditions were much worse under the Americans than they had been under Jerry. Nothing was written about this at the time because of the censors. Nothing will be written now because it is water under the dam."

"After we were liberated," Blackmon remembered, "everybody just went where they wanted to go. We just went on our merry way; we went to a small village and there comes a guy rushing out of a house, a Russian prisoner, skin and bones with a whole sack of flour on his back and a housewife running out after him calling in German about 'kinder, kinder,' she had children. She was trying to beat him with a broom. Frank 'Ace' Scorsune got the flour back to her."

Back in the States, with the memories of liberation from Stalag XVII still fresh in his mind, Blackmon headed downtown to the fanciest hotel in New Orleans, The Roosevelt, to have some fun in the town's French Quarter. With its elegant ceilings, chandeliers, and live Dixieland Jazz music, it was the ideal place to celebrate coming home. In the middle of the ornate lobby, he spotted a pretty blonde girl on the arm of an Army officer and had to look twice before he recognized the face of his sister, Katie. Her eyes brightened when she saw her brother and she ran into his arms.

A newly released soldier with a bit of a swagger left in him, Bill Blackmon embraced his sister and pulled out a twenty dollar bill to give her, a large sum of money in 1945. Perhaps it was also to let her companion know that Katie had an older brother who was looking out for her.

"Does Mama know you're back?" asked Katie. "She's been waiting at the train station for four hours."

"She left me waiting four and a half years," he said, remembering that cloud of dust behind their mother's car as she left the orphanage back in 1932.

When he saw his mother later that day, she told him that during his capture, she had imagined parachuting down into Stalag XVII just to be with him. He grinned at the idea of his mother joining him behind the barbed wire. "If she'd have done that, I'd have been the laughingstock of the whole place. I'd have escaped and run all the way to Switzerland!"

Once he'd settled back in Louisiana, Blackmon bought a used car, a gray 1940 Chevrolet Club Coupe, the Special Deluxe model. He had a score to settle with the man who had tormented him at the orphanage, the husband of the matron, Una. This was the one who had humiliated him after he'd wet the bed when he was eight, forcing him to wear a diaper and stand in public with his urine-soaked bed clothing. Many nights he had fallen asleep with bruises on his back and legs from the vicious beatings the man had delivered. "They'd beat you hard," Blackmon remembered. "Even for something like throwing a field pea at another kid when we were all out in the fields, working."

While a buddy from the service named Nelson Johnson kept Bill's Chevrolet Club Coupe running outside, with a quick get-away planned, Blackmon tracked down his former tormenter at the hardware store. He found him working at a back counter, a balding man who'd grown thin and stooped in the intervening years.

"Do you know me?" Bill, who had always been gangly and tall, towered over him now, glaring.

He looked up and shook his head. "No, son, I don't."

"I'm Bill Blackmon."

The hateful face that Blackmon remembered from the orphanage lit up in a delighted smile of recognition. "We saw your picture in the newspaper when you were captured. Una and me, we prayed for you to come home. Thank god you're alive! It's good to have you back, son."

Blackmon laughed at the memory. "Instead of punching him out, I bought a buck knife from him for sixteen dollars. I walked out to where my buddy Nelson sat at the wheel of my new car. He said, 'So did you beat him up?' And I says, 'Hell no, I bought this knife from him.' I still have that knife. Every time I look at it, I think about those cold water baths and urine-soaked sheets and him, praying for me during the war." He paused. "You know, I don't have as many dreams about being a POW as I do about the orphanage—sometimes I dream I'm back there, trying to escape."

But those awful years of waiting for either escape or rescue had, in some terrible way, taught him bitter lessons of survival that served him in Stalag XVII. Remarkably, Bill Blackmon never lost his sense of justice and compassion along the way.

Afterword

In his self-portrait of a World War II radioman, Claudio Stefano Carano turns his back to us as he goes about the warrior's job at hand. His radio controls are temporarily forgotten as he aims a machine gun directly at an oncoming German bomber, while another swooshes upward into the distant sky. The vision appears dizzying, yet his feet are planted steadily, his eyes focused on his enemy. Instead, he gives us the faces of his comrades: the chiseled slant of Slim Lassater's cheek in semiprofile, the determined jut of Joe Hafer's chin, perhaps fresh off a win in the boxing ring, Kurt Kurtenbach's gaze, steady, deliberate, somewhat introspective. Carano gives us the chillingly spare gray lines that compose Stalag XVII's barracks and guard towers, the red warmth of the chapel services led in Reverend Stephen Kane's Irish brogue at Easter, the silvery motion of B-17s against European skies, and the quilt of Nazi-held countryside, silent and waiting, beneath.

A mosaic emerges in Carano's pages: his drawings put in the foreground his comrades and the icons of his survival, whether plane or barrack or the face of a friend or family member. The pages also document the stark reality of what he survived—and how he survived it. Community was one essential element, the trust of comrades, the letters from distant family. Confidence was another means of survival, a sense of oneself in the solitude of one's bunk, the spiritual and creative empowerment that allowed one to be safe in one's self. Mission was yet another means of survival: knowledge of a cause worth fighting, faith in leaders on all levels such as Kurtenbach, Eisenhower, and Roosevelt. Each piece formed a larger whole.

Violently plucked from the sky, prisoners of war suffered fates dependent on when and where they were captured: those like Carano and Bill Blackmon were relatively fortunate—if the word "fortunate" can ever describe them—to have survived the experience in a single camp, with a somewhat predictable set of routines and an established group of comrades in the same barracks. Others, like John Bitzer and my uncle, Bill Davidge, were yanked from one camp to another and endured what would later be deemed war crimes: crowded into the suffocating, dark hold of a steamship for a two-day journey to another stalag, chased by German Shepard dogs and bayoneted as Germans forced the prisoners to run three kilometers to the new camp, then march six hundred miles until, months later, they met freedom in the faces of fellow American GIs. Given the circumstances under which John Bitzer carried his wartime log, it is amazing that it survived at all.

The legacy left behind by Claudio Stefano Carano and John C. Bitzer in their journals paid homage to men in stalags all over Nazi-held Europe, not only by recording their stories and their faces, but by exemplifying the creative means they found to survive a terrible ordeal. The journals provided a forum for the men to write their own essays and poetry. The subject could be either the mundane or the sentimentally sublime—what mattered to Carano in particular was the sense of camaraderie that emerged from the theater of his journal. In those pages, he created both a private retreat for himself and a public space for his friends, a kind of garden that he could cultivate and nourish. In some prison camps, the men kept literal gardens, tilling dry dirt and tending the life of withered carrot sticks— a measuring of time, a comforting ritual that meant more than the few calories they would reap from their efforts. In a similar way, the journals kept alive hope. They, too, were a way of tending life and of measuring the seamless stretch of prison time, carving it into words and pages. The POWs who took up the offer of these journals and art supplies answered an invitation to create their own worlds and, in so doing, they might feel, however briefly, that they had control over an uncertain environment in which they had little power. They turned their diaries into objects of art, a treasure in a place where valued possessions were few.

For the prisoners who kept journals, writing and drawing became ways of taking up arms to empower themselves, of reminding themselves that they were recording facts and details for the "real" history, the truth, that would survive the propaganda distributed by the "Jerries" who guarded their camps and censored their mail. In a world where the only mirrors were in other men's eyes, such creations must have become extensions of themselves, a way of shoring up one's identity.

A great creative spirit was kindled by the blank pages of these books. In the German stalags, they empowered the men who put pencil to paper and invested their thoughts and feelings there, making invaluable records not only of history but of how the imagination survives the worst nightmares, and triumphs with intelligence, dignity and humor.

The YMCA books suggested that the men could create order and even beauty in a world gone horribly wrong. They served as a kind of tabula rasa for the human spirit under some of the greatest stresses of endurance. What they reveal is the survival of creativity and confidence, and the enduring will to wrest meaning, and even art, from chaos.

Those accomplishments, whatever form they took, helped many of the men of the German stalags endure the hunger, brutal cold, and, perhaps worst of all, the uncertainty of the future in a Nazi prison camp. They accomplished many wartime feats not only aboard their "Flying Fortresses" in those daring raids over Germany, but also in a solitary place that only the prisoners of war came to know during the hungry, cold months under the watch of often brutal guards. It was a feat of personal survival not understood by many Americans, who were eager to hear stories of grand adventure after the war's end. After capture, theirs was not a tale of glorified heroics, but a story of keeping body, mind, and soul alive under grueling uncertainty and tedium—a heroism of the spirit that is often forgotten.

Further Readings

The list of books about World War II is continually growing. As aging veterans put together their memoirs, the body of work on prisoners of war and personal wartime experience expands in rich new directions. The suggestions below are not intended, by any means, to be definitive, but are a starting point for readers in search of information and new insights about the most terrible war of our time.

Ahlbrandt, William Laird Kleine. *Bitter Prerequisites. A Faculty for Survival from Nazi Terror.* Lafayette, IN: Purdue University Press, 1992.

Ash, William, with Brendan Foley. *Under the Wire: The World War II Adventures of a Legendary Escape Artist and "Cooler King."* New York: Thomas Dunne Books, 2005.

Bard, Mitchell G. *Forgotten Victims: The Abandonment of Americans in Hitler's Camps.* Boulder, CO: Westview Press, 1994.

Barker, A. J. *Prisoners of War.* New York: Universe Books, 1975.

Baron, Richard, Abe Baum, and Richard Goldhurst. *Raid! The Untold Story of Patton's Secret Mission.* New York: G. P. Putnam's Sons, 1981.

Beltrone, Art and Lee Beltrone. *A Wartime Log.* Charlottesville, VA: Howell Press, 1995.

Bird, Tom. *American POWs of World War II: Forgotten Men Tell Their Stories.* Westport, CT: Praeger Publishers,1992.

Brickhill, Paul. *The Great Escape.* Greenwich, CN: Faber, 1950.

Bunyak, Dawn Trimble. *Our Last Mission: A World War II Prisoner in Germany.* Norman: University of Oklahoma Press, 2003.

Burgess, Alan. *The Longest Tunnel: the True Story of World War II's Great Escape.* New York: Grove Weidenfeld, 1990.

Carlson, Lewis H. *We Were Each Other's Prisoners.* New York: Basic Books. 1997.

————, Ed., with Angelo M. Spinelli. *Life Behind Barbed Wire: The Secret World War II Photographs of Angelo M. Spinelli.* New York: Fordham University Press 2004.

Carroll, Tim. *The Great Escape from Stalag Luft III: The Full Story of How 76 Allied Officers Carried Out World War II's Most Remarkable Mass Escape.* New York: Pocket Books, 2005.

Chiesl, O. M. *Clipped Wings.* Dayton, OH: R. W. Kimball, 1948.

Clark, Albert P. *33 Months As A POW in Stalag Luft III: A WWII Airman Tells His Story.* Golden, CO: Fulcrum 2005.

Cohen, Bernard M. and Cooper, Maurice Z. *A Follow-Up Study of World War II Prisoners of War.* Washington, DC: U.S. Government Printing Office, 1954.

Cohen, Roger. *Soldiers and Slaves: American POWs Trapped by the Nazis.* New York: Knopf, 2005.

Collins, Douglas. *POW.* New York: Norton, 1968.

Cox, Luther. *Always Fighting the Enemy.* Baltimore: Gateway Press, 1990.

Crosby, Harry H. *A Wing and A Prayer: The "Bloody 100th" Bomb Group of the U.S. Eighth Air Force in Action Over Europe in World War II.* New York: HarperCollins, 1993.

Daniel, Eugene L. *In the Presence of Mine Enemies: An American Chaplain in World War II German Prison Camps.* Charlotte, NC: E. L. Daniel, 1985.

Davis, George, J. *The Hitler Diet, As Inflicted on American POWs in World War II.* Los Angeles: Military Literary Guild, 1990.

Daws, Gavin. *Prisoners of the Japanese: POWs of World War II in the Pacific.* New York: William Morrow, 1994.

Des Pres, Terrence. *The Survivor: An Anatomy of Life in the Death Camps.* New York: Oxford University Press, 1976.

Diggs, J. Frank. *Americans Behind the Wire: World War II: Inside a German Prison Camp.* Saint Petersburg, FL: Vandamere Press, 2000.

Dobran, Edward. *P.O.W.* New York: Exposition Press, 1953.

Doyle, Robert. *A Prisoner's Duty: Great Escapes in U.S. Military History.* Annapolis: Naval Institute Press, 1997.

Doyle, Robert C. *Voices of Captivity: Interpreting the American POW Narrative.* Lawrence: University Press of Kansas, 1994.

Drooz, Daniel B. *American Prisoners of War in German Death, Concentration, and Slave Labor Camps.* Lewiston, NY: Mellon Press, 2003.

Duke, Florimond. *Name, Rank, and Serial Number.* New York: Meredith Press, 1969.

Durand, Arthur A. *Stalag Luft III: The Secret Story.* Baton Rouge: Louisiana State University Press, 1988.

Ferguson, Clarence. *Kriegsgefangener 3024, POW.* Waco, TX: Texian Press, 1983.

Foy, David A. *For You the War Is Over: American POWs in Nazi Germany.* New York: Stein & Day, 1984.

Franklin, H. Bruce. *M.I.A. or Mythmaking in America.* Brooklyn, NY: Lawrence Hill Books, 1992.

Frelinghuysen, Joe. *Passages to Freedom.* Manhattan, KS: Sunflower University Press, 1990.

Fussell, Paul. *Wartime: Understanding and Behavior in the Second World War.* New York : Oxford University Press, 1989.

Greening, Col. Charles Ross, Dorothy Greening, and Karen Morgan Driscoll. *Not As Briefed: From the Doolittle Raid to a German Stalag.* Vancouver: University of British Columbia Press, 2004.

Halmos, Eugene E. Jr. *The Wrong Side of the Fence: A United States Army Corps POW in World War II.* Shippensberg, PA: White Mane Publishers, 1996.

Hamann, Lorin W. *A Prisoner Remembers World War II.* Elkader, IA: L. W. Hamann, 1984.

Handy, Ned and Kemp Battle. *The Flame Keepers: The True Story of an American Soldier's Survival Inside Stalag 17.* New York: Hyperion, 2004.

Harrison, Jack S. *Flight from Youth: the Story of an American POW.* Madison, WI: J. S. Harrison, 1973.

Harsh, George. *Lonesome Road.* New York: W. W. Norton & Co., 1971.

Hatch, Gardner, Ed. *American Ex-POWs.* Paducah, KY: Turner Publishers, 1988.

Helphand, Kenneth I. *Defiant Gardens: Making Gardens in Wartime.* San Antonio, TX: Trinity University Press, 2006.

Higgins, Sam. *Survival: Diary of an American POW in World War II.* PSI Research/L&R Publishing, 2000.

Homze, Edward. *Foreign Labor in Nazi Germany.* Princeton, NJ: Princeton Uni. Press, 1967.

Hopewell, Clifford. *Combine 13.* Dallas: Merrimore Press, 1990.

Howell, Forrest W. *Whispers of Death: Yankee Kriegies.* Moore Haven, FL: Rainbow Books, 1985.

Irving, David John Cawdell. *The Destruction of Dresden.* New York: Ballentine Books, 1985.

Jackson, Charles R. and Bruce H. Norton, Ed. *I Am Alive! A United States Marine's Story of Survival in a World War II Japanese POW Camp.* New York: Ballantine Books, 2003.

Jefferson, Alexander, with Lewis H. Carlson. *Red Tail Captured, Red Tail Free: The Memoirs of a Tuskegee Airman and POW.* New York: Fordham University Press, 2005.

Kehlenhofer, Guy L. *Understanding the former Prisoner of War: Life after Liberation.* St. Paul, MN: Banfil Street Press, 1992.

Lister, Hal. *Krautland Calling: An American POW Radio Broadcaster in Nazi Germany.* Austin, TX: Eakin Press, 1989.

Meltesen, Clarence R. *Roads to Liberation.* San Francisco: Oflag 64 Press, 1990.

Mills, Irving J. "Eagles Can Walk." Unpublished log of march and liberation. 1946.

Moore, Bob, Ed. *Prisoners-of-War and Their Captors in World War II.* London: Berg, 1996.

Morgan, Col. Robert, with Ron Powers. *The Man Who Flew the Memphis Belle, Memoir of a World War II Bomber Pilot.* New York: Dutton, 2001.

Motley, Mary Penick, Ed. *The Invisible Soldier: The Experiences of the Black Soldier, World War II.* Detroit: Wayne State University Press, 1975.

Myers, Jack R. *Shot At and Missed: Recollections of a World War II Bombardier.* Norman: University of Oklahoma Press, 2004.

Newcomb, Alan. *Vacation with Pay: Being an Account of My Stay at the German Rest Camp for Tired Allied Airmen at Beautiful Barth-on-the-Baltic (Stalag Luft 1).* Haverhill, MA: Destiny Publishers, 1947.

Nichol, John and Tony Rennell. *The Last Escape: The Untold Story of Allied Prisoners of War in Europe 1944–45.* New York: Viking, 2002.

O'Donnell, Joseph P. *The Shoe Leather Express: The Evacuation of Kriegsgefangener Lager Stalag Luft IV, Deutschland, Germany.* Robbinsville, NJ: J. P. O'Donnell, 1982.

———. *Luftgangsters.* Robbinsville, NJ: J. P. O'Donnell, 1982.

Pitts, Jesse Richard. *Return to Base: Memoirs of a B-17 Copilot, Kimbolton, England, 1943–1944.* Chalottesville, VA: Howell Press 2004.

Rasmussen, Randall L. *Hell's Belle, from a B-17 to Stalag XVII B: Based on the Memoirs of William Rasmussen.* Santa Fe, NM: Sunstone Press, 2003.

Sage, Colonel Jerry. *The Man the Germans Could Not Keep Prisoner.* Wayne, PA: Miles Standish Press, 1985.

Sampson, Francis. *Paratrooper Padre.* Washington, DC: Catholic University of America Press, 1948.

Sexton, Winton K. *Back Roads to Freedom.* Kansas City, MO: Lowell Press, 1985.

Shoemaker, Lloyd R. *The Escape Factory.* New York: St. Martin's Press, 1990.

Spach, Jules C. *Every Road Leads Home: Memoirs of Jule C. Spach, POW-World War II.* Professional Publishing 1996.

Spiller, Harry. *Prisoners of Nazis: Accounts by American POWs in World War II.* Jefferson, N.C.: McFarland and Company, 1997.

Spivey, Delmar. *POW Odyssey: Recollections of Center Compound, Stalag Luft III and the Secret German Peace Mission in World War II.* Attleboro, MA: Colonial Lithograph, 1984.

Stevens, Charles N. *An Innocent at Polebrook: A Memoir of an 8th Air Force Bombardier.* Bloomington, IN: Authorhouse, 2004.

Stone, James F. *A Holiday in Hitlerland.* New York: Carlton Press, 1970.

Terkel, Studs. *The Good War: An Oral History of World War II.* New York: Pantheon, 1984.

Vietor, John A. *Time Out: American Airmen at Stalag Luft 1.* Fallbrook, CA: Aero Publishing, 1984.

Vulliet, Andre. *The YMCA and Prisoners of War During World War II.* Geneva: International Committee of the YMCA, 1946.

Weingartner, James. *Crossroads of Death: the Story of the Malmedy Massacre and Trial*. Berkeley: University of California Press, 1979.

Westheimer, David. *Sitting It Out: A World War II POW Memoir*. Houston: Rice University Press. 1992.

Wolter, Tim. *POW Baseball in World War II: The National Pastime Behind Barbed Wire*. Jefferson, NC: McFarland & Co., 2001.

Wright, Stuart J. *An Emotional Gauntlet: From Life in Peacetime America to the War in European Skies*. Madison: University of Wisconsin Press, 2004.

Zemke, Hubert. *Zemke's Stalag: The Final Days of World War II*. Washington, DC: Smithsonian Institution, 1991.

Zemke, Hubert. *Zemke's Wolf Pack*. New York: Pocket Books, 1988.

INDEX

Page numbers in italics refer to illustrations.

A

American Ex-POWs Association, 16,
  112, 136
Army Air Corps, 7, 22, 108, 128, 133

B

B-17, ix, xv, xvi, 7, 8, 10, 28, *Y,* 133, 135,
  137, 147
B-24, 137
ball turret gunner, xvi, 54, 108–9
"Baltic Cruise," xxi, 110, 112, 116–18.
  See also war crimes, Nazi
Bang, Charles, 13–14, 44, 101, *E–F*
barb-wire psychosis, xi
Battle of the Bulge, The, 12, 141
BBC news, 12, 76
Berlin blitz, 11, 135
Bitzer, John C., x, xvi, xvii, xix, xx,
  xxi, *Y,* 105–16, 123, 125, 148
Bitzer, Marian, xix, *Y*
black market, 55
Blackmon, William H., x, xi, xv, xix,
  6, 7, 8–9, 11–13, 16, 25, 36, *A,*
  127–46
blitzkrieg, Polish, 73
bomb group, 381st, 7
bomb squadron, 535th, 7

C

Carano, Claudio Stephen, x, xi, xiii,
  xiv, xvi, xvii, 5, 6, 7, 9, 12, 13, 14, 15,
  16, 20, 21, 45, 73, *A–B,* 107, 134,
  140, 147–48
Carano, Rose, xiv, xix, xx, 5, 9–10, 13,
  16, 44, *E*
Carlson, Lewis, xi, xx, 151, 156
Casablanca Conference, ix
Clark, Arthur, xv, xvi
Cologne, Germany, 28, 35, *L*
Cordner, John, xiv
Culver, Charles, 27, 36, 98, 101, *X,* 107

D

D-Day invasion, 12
Davidge, William F., v, xv, xvii, xxi, *Y,*
  138, 148
death march, Baltic, xvi, xvii, xxi, 107,
  111–12. *See also* war crimes, Nazi
denunciations of POWs by American
  citizens, 16, 66–68
Der Adler, 91
Dulag Luft, Frankfurt, 34, 64, 64, 109,
  137–38

E

Early, Charles, xiv
Eighth Army Air Force, 7, 8, 10
female impersonation shows, prisoner
  of war, 14, 77, *U*
escape plans, prisoner of war, 13–14,
  21, 42, 44–45, 48, 65, *E–F, I,*
  140–41

F

Ferrino, Walter "Chic," 79, 81, 83, *X*
Flying Fortress, 8, 149
Focke-Wulf 190, 68, 133, 135
food and diet, POW, xiv, 11, 36, 39, 40, 41, 46–47, 59, 60, 61–62, 63–64, 98, 109, 111, 143
French resistance, 50–58, 112–37
Friesen Islands, 26

G

Geneva Convention, The, x, 11, 37, 40, 42, *R*
Gestapo, 53–55, 57
Gordon, Lee C. (actual), *U,* 134–35, 139–40
Gordon, Lee C. (imposter), 88–89, *T, U,* 139
Gross Tychow Pomerania, 113
Groth, Charles, 13, 36, 44, 102, *E–F, K, X*
guards, German prison, 14, 39, 41–42, 78, 110, *Q, W,* 138–39, 141–42, 144–45

H

Hafer, Joseph, 41, 65, 102, *I,* 147
Handy, Ned, 144, 153
Healy, L., 32, *D*
Henslin, 26, 28
Heydekrug Run, The, xxi, 110–12. *See also* war crimes, Nazi
Himmler, Heinrich, ix
Hitler, Adolph, 11, 35, 142
Hodges, Courtney Hicks, First Army, 115
humor, prisoner of war, xiv, 32, 46, 47, 88–89, *T–W,* 141

I

International Red Cross. *See* Red Cross

J

Jewish death camp victims, 142–43
Josephson, Carlton, 13–14, 27–29, 31–32, 44, *E–F, X*

K

Kane, Stephen W., 15, 73–76, 147
Kilroy cartoon, 138
Krems, Austria, 11, 35, 43, 64, 142
Kriegies, 11, 12, 15, 35, 64, 68, 76, 95
Kuptsow, Aaron, xiv
Kurtenbach, Kenneth "Kurt," 38, 71, *G, S,* 139, 147

L

Lassiter, Joseph E. "Slim," 15, 48–64, 103, *H,* 147
liberation from Nazis, xvii, 16, 97–98, 107–8, 112, 113–15, 142–45
liberation march to Branau, Germany, 17, 97–98
Lieberman, Roke, xx, 73
Luftgangster, ix, 35
Luftwaffe, German, 8, 49

M

"Mae West" life preserver, 50
Man of Confidence. *See* Kenneth "Kurt" Kurtenbach
MC-110, 108
McCutchen, D. C., 26–29, 32, *D*
ME-109, 31, 135
Mecklenburg, 142
Mills, Irving J., 143, 145, 153

N

nurses, Dutch, 10, 99

O

orphanage, Louisiana methodist, xv, 7, 129–33, 142, 146

P

Parises Zeitgung, 95
Pearl Harbor, attack on, 10
Pettus, Carl, *J*
Phelper, Ben, 15
poetry, POW, xiv, xvi, 14, 25, 58, 66, 68, 71–72, 76–87, 116–25, 138, 148
POW WOW, xiii, 76
prisoners of war, American Jewish, 73
prisoners of war, French, 37–39
prisoners of war, Italian, 36, 37, 39, *R*
prisoners of war, Russian, 11, 36, 37, 40, *R,* 140
propaganda, German, 15, 35, 66, 91–94
propaganda, U.S., 95–96

R

radio gunner, operator, 7, 10, 26, 49, 62, 65, 134
radio, wireless, 10, 12, 76, *N,* 139, 141
rations, wartime, 55
Red Cross, x, xiii, 13, 25, 39, 40, *C*
Red Cross food parcels, x, xiv, 11, 34, 36, 42, 46, 82–83, *S,* 109, 111, 140
Red Cross parcels, sporting equipment, 41–42
religious services, Stalag XVII B, 73–76, *S*
Rembur, Pieret, xvi, xix, *Y*
Resistance Documentation Center, Luxembourg, xx
Ridgewell Air Force Base, 7, 8, 10, 133–35,
Roosevelt, Franklin Delano, 12

S

sports and sporting equipment, prisoner of war, x, 14, 41–42, 72
Stalag XIA, 113
Stalag XVII-B, xiii, xiv, xix, xx, 6, 10, 11, 17, 21, 25, 35, 42–43, 64, 66, 71, *M,* 128–29, 134–35, 142–45, 147
Stalag XVII-B (film and play), xiii, 14
Stalag Luft III B, xiii
Stalag Luft I, xiv, xx
Stalag Luft IV, xvi, 107, 111–12, 114
Stalag Luft VI, xvi, 107, 109–110, 112, 116, 118
Stalin, Josef, 11, 37
Stebbing, Frank, 76, 80, 82, 86–87
storm troopers, Nazi, 15, 142, 144
suicides, POW, 21, 139–40
Sunde, P. H. V., 26–28, 30, 32, *D*
Swartz, Robert, xiv

T

Terrorflieger, ix, 137
Third Reich, ix, 133

W

war crimes, Nazi , xxi, 110–11, 117, 148
Wartime Log. *See* YMCA Wartime Log
Wissous, France, xx, xxi, *Y*
Wissous, France, World War II Remembrance Service, xv, xvi, xvii, xix, xx, *Y*

Y

YMCA, x, xiii, 13, 41
YMCA, wartime log, xiii, xvi, xvii, xix, 13, 14, 25, *C,* 107–8, 110, 129, 148–49

KAY SLOAN is professor of English at Miami University in Ohio. She is the author of *The Loud Silents: Origins of the Social Problem Film* and, with William H. Goetzmann, *Looking Far North: The Harriman Expedition to Alaska, 1899.* She is the author of two novels, including *The Patron Saint of Red Chevys,* a Barnes & Noble "Discover Great New Writers" selection, and a poetry collection, *The Birds Are on Fire,* winner of the New Women's Voices Prize. She is also the coeditor of the fiction anthology *Elvis Rising* and the producer and director of a documentary, *Suffragettes in the Silent Cinema.*

LEWIS H. CARLSON is professor emeritus of history at Western Michigan University and the author of *We Were Each Other's Prisoners: An Oral History of World War II American and German Prisoners of War.*